Ambrose Yeomans Moore

History of the Presbytery of Indianapolis

Ambrose Yeomans Moore

History of the Presbytery of Indianapolis

ISBN/EAN: 9783337293130

Printed in Europe, USA, Canada, Australia, Japan

Cover: Foto ©ninafisch / pixelio.de

More available books at **www.hansebooks.com**

OF

The Presbytery of Indianapolis.

BY

A. Y. MOORE.

PUBLISHED BY THE PRESBYTERY.

INDIANAPOLIS:
JOHN G. DOUGHTY, PRINTER, CORNER MERIDIAN AND CIRCLE STREETS.
1876.

EXTRACT from the Minutes of the Presbytery of Indianapolis, in session at Greenwood, September, 1875:

"Rev. A. Y. MOORE was chosen to prepare a History of the Presbytery, to be read at the Spring meeting."

Extract from the Minutes of Presbytery, in session at Southport, April, 1876:

"Rev. A. Y. MOORE read a part of the History he had prepared of this Presbytery, and he was requested to complete the History, and prepare it for publication."

CONTENTS.

CHAPTER I.

Church at Bloomington—Rev. Isaac Reed—Bible Society—First Preaching in Indiana—First Churches—Early Times—The State Capital is located and named—Organization of Church at Indianapolis—Chronological Comparisons......... 1

CHAPTER II.

Louisville and Salem Presbyteries—Indianapolis as a Missionary Field—First Ordination in the State—Ordination and Installation at Bloomington—Organization of Churches at Columbus, Franklin, Greencastle, and Greenwood—Presbytery of Wabash—Synod of Indiana—Difficulties with Mr. Bush—Presbytery of Crawfordsville—Difficulties in Presbytery—Difficulties Allayed....................................... 16

CHAPTER III.

Presbytery of Indianapolis—First Statistical Report—The Field and its Occupation in 1830—Decision of Presbytery on Representation, Presbytery Resisting Division—Complaint against Presbytery—Dissensions from Diversity in Doctrine—Items—Hopewell—Industrial Aspects and Interests—Southport, Danville, Greencastle, Shiloh, Bethany—The Field at the time of the Great Division of the Church.. 27

CONTENTS.

CHAPTER IV.

Action of the Presbytery of Indianapolis in the Great Division of the Church—Action of the Presbytery of Crawfordsville—Greencastle First—Greencastle Second—Putnamville, Poplar Spring, Bainbridge, Carpentersville, Bloomington, Columbus.. 43

CHAPTER V.

Second Church of Indianapolis—Indianapolis Presbytery, N. S.—Enlargement of Presbytery—Ministerial Changes—Changes in Churches—Missionary Work—Pastoral Relation—Report to General Assembly.. 50

CHAPTER VI.

Presbytery of Indianapolis, O. S.—Churches Organized—Ministerial Changes—Lessons from the History of Franklin Church—Ministerial Support—Missionary Work—Organization of White Water Presbytery, and Changes in the Boundaries of the Presbytery... 59

CHAPTER VII.

View of the Field from Reports of Indiana Gazetteer—Number of Old and New School Churches, and their Increase in Membership—Progress and Prosperity of the Country.. 71

CHAPTER VIII.

Indianapolis Presbytery, O. S.—Changes in Churches—Ministerial Changes—State of Religion—Missionary Work—Presbyterial Authority—First Church of Indianapolis—Second Church of Greencastle—Numbers.. 74

CHAPTER IX.

Indianapolis Presbytery, N. S.—New Churches—Second Church of Indianapolis—Fourth Church of Indianapolis—Greenwood—Ministerial Changes—Missionary Work—Danville, White Lick, Greencastle, Putnamville, Bainbridge, Bloomington, Columbus.. 83

CHAPTER X.

Numbers—Census Report of the Statistics of the different Denominations in the Field of the Presbytery...................... 92

CHAPTER XI.

Indianapolis Presbytery, N. S.—Greenfield Church—Kingston and Clarksburg—Edinburg—Sixth Church of Indianapolis —Shelbyville—Ministerial Changes—Progress— Reunion— Adjournment *sine die*—Hendricks County—Putnam County —Bloomington—Columbus—Numbers............................. 96

CHAPTER XII.

Indianapolis Presbytery, O. S.—Changes in Churches—Ministerial Changes—Deaths—State of the Country—Revivals— Reunion—First Church at Indianapolis—Seventh Church at Indianapolis—Brownsburg and Clermont—Greencastle, Carpentersville, Bloomington—Numbers........................... 107

CHAPTER XIII.

Indianapolis Presbytery — Its Boundaries, Members and Churches—Changes in Churches—Ministerial Changes— Missionary Work—Woman's Presbyterial Society—Revivals 119

HISTORY

OF THE

PRESBYTERY OF INDIANAPOLIS.

CHAPTER I.

Church at Bloomington—Rev. Isaac Reed—Bible Society—First Preaching in Indiana—First Churches—Early Times—The State Capital located and named—Organization of Church at Indianapolis—Chronological Comparisons.

1805—1823.

THE Presbytery of Indianapolis comprises within its limits the following counties: Putnam, Hendricks, Marion, Hancock, Johnson, Morgan, Monroe, Brown and Bartholomew.

The oldest Presbyterian church within this district is that of Bloomington, Monroe county. This church was organized the 27th of September, 1819. One year before this all the rest of the territory now included within the bounds of the Presbytery of Indianapolis, except Monroe county, was in the possession of the Indians. At St. Mary's, Ohio, a treaty was made upon the 3d of October, 1818, by the government of the United States with the Delaware Indians, who then occupied this territory, by which they transferred it to the United States. In the treaty, the right was reserved to the Indians of remaining in the country, and occupying it as a hunting ground for three years; after this they were to be removed by the government of the United States to territory assigned to them west of the Mississippi.* This tract of country purchased from the Delawares was called, in the settlement of the country, the New Purchase, and known as such.

The county of Monroe was partly within the limits of the New Purchase and partly within the limits of a purchase made of the Indians by General Harrison at Ft. Wayne in 1809; a purchase which was one of the chief causes that stirred up the hostility of Tecumseh and his brother, the Shawnee Prophet, and led to the Indian war, which was begun with the battle of Tippecanoe, November 7th, 1811.

The enabling act of Congress which made Indiana a State in 1816, devolved upon James Monroe, the President of the United States, the duty of setting apart a township of land for University purposes, in addition to the township that had been already granted to the University of Vincennes. The President designated for the State University a township of land in what afterwards became Monroe county. Doubtless this assignment of land for University purposes led to the speedy settlement and organization of Monroe county. The county of Monroe, which was previously a part of Orange county, with the county seat at Paoli, was organized by the Legislature of 1818. The county seat was located April 11th, 1818, and named Bloomington. This was

* Dillon's Indiana, p. 575.

six months before the acquisition of the New Purchase from the Delawares.

The first entrance of a Presbyterian or Congregational minister within the boundaries of this presbytery was, in all probability, made in the fall of 1818. The Rev. Orin Fowler, who spent a year in the State under the direction of the Connecticut Missionary Society, visited Bloomington in the fall of 1818. Mr. Fowler thus writes from Carlisle, in Sullivan county, to Rev. Isaac Reed, then preaching at New Albany: "I have been on a tour to Monroe county, (Bloomington county seat), which was very fatiguing; have been up the Wabash river to Fort Harrison (Terre Haute), and preached in nearly every neighborhood in these several directions."*

In the fall of 1819 the Rev. Isaac Reed, who was then preaching for the church of New Albany, made a missionary tour into the interior of the State to distribute Bibles and to preach. The Bibles, he says, were the remains of a society which had been formed at Jeffersonville by the agency of the Rev. Samuel J. Mills and the Rev. Daniel Smith, during the days of the territorial existence of Indiana, and while Colonel Posey was Governor. In 1814, Samuel J. Mills and Daniel Smith, under the combined patronage of the Connecticut and Massachusetts Missionary Societies, made a journey through the States and Territories of the southwest, preaching and organizing Bible and other benevolent societies. In November of this year, these men visited St. Louis, and "preached the first sermons ever heard from ministers of their denomination in that French village."† It was to distribute the Bibles of this Bible Society, organized

*Reed's Christian Traveller, p. 97.
†Sprague's Annals of the Presbyterian Pulpit, Vol. IV, p. 506.

at Jeffersonville by Samuel J. Mills and his colaborer, Daniel Smith, and to preach the gospel " in the regions beyond," that the Rev. Isaac Reed made, in the fall of 1819, a missionary tour " as far as to the frontier counties of Monroe and Owen." By this thread of influence, slight, yet real, and most interesting and precious, the organization of the oldest church of the presbytery becomes associated with the life and labors of one " whose praise is in all the churches," and to whom is largely due the organization both of the American Board of Missions and the American Bible Society.

The church at Bloomington was " the first church," says Mr. Reed, " formed by my ministry."* Mr. Reed became a veteran missionary, and probably organized more churches in the State than any other man.†

The first record we have of a Presbyterian minister preaching within the limits of Indiana, is of Thomas Cleland, of Kentucky. In the Life of Dr. Cleland we find the following:

" Transylvania Presbytery had no definite limits in a southern direction; it also included Indiana, etc., on the north. In the spring of 1805 I was directed to visit Vincennes and the adjoining regions. It was an uninhabited route I had to go. A small wilderness trace, with only one residence on the way, in the most destitute part of the way, to entertain me during the night. Here was my poor animal tied to a tree, fed with the grain packed in a wallet from Louisville, and myself stretched on the puncheon floor of a small cabin, for the night's rest. All passed off, however, without any detriment or discomfort. The next evening made up for all previous privations. I was welcomed and agreeably

*Christian Traveller, p. 93.
†Historical Discourse, by Rev. J. H. Johnston.

entertained at the Governor's palace during my stay in Vincennes. The late William Henry Harrison, then a young man, with a Presbyterian wife, was Governor of the Indiana Territory, as it then was. He had recently held a treaty with a certain tribe of Indians, who assembled at Vincennes.

"The first sermon I preached—and it was the first ever preached in the place, at least by a Presbyterian minister—was in the council house, but a short time before occupied by the sons of the forest. I preached also in a settlement twenty miles up the Wabash, where were a few Presbyterian families, chiefly from Shelby county, Kentucky."*

It is possible that in Clarke county, which Governor Harrison established by proclamation February 3, 1801, there may have been preaching, either by some Presbyterian or other minister, earlier than the time mentioned by Mr. Cleland, when he preached at Vincennes.

In the Minutes of the General Assembly for 1805, we find that about the time Cleland is threading his way through the wilderness to Vincennes, Mr. Thomas Williamson, a licentiate of the Second Presbytery of South Carolina, is appointed to spend three months in missionary services, "in the lower parts of the State of Ohio, and in the Indian Territory as low as Kaskaskia."

By Indian Territory in this minute of the Assembly we must understand Indiana Territory, which was organized in 1800, and embraced all the territory of the country west of Ohio, and north of the Ohio river. When, in 1803, the Lousiana purchase was made, all of the territory west of the Mississippi, and as far south as the southern boundary of Arkansas, was added to the

---

* Life of Dr. Cleland—Moore Wilstach, Keys & Co., Cincinnati, 1859, p. 87.

territorial government of Indiana. In 1805, the territorial governments of Missouri and of Michigan were organized. But it was not until 1809, that the Territory of Illinois was established by detaching from the Territory of Indiana the country which is now embraced in the States of Illinois and Wisconsin, and that part of Minnesota which lies east of the Mississippi. In the Minutes of the Assembly for 1806, we find this resolution: "That Mr. Samuel Scott, of the Presbytery of West Lexington, be a Missionary for three months, in the Indiana Territory, and especially at Vincennes."

In Mr. Dickey's Brief History, this is the year of the date of the organization of the Indiana church, the first Presbyterian church organized in Indiana The second church organized, was one in the vicinity of Charlestown, Clarke county, called Palmyra. It was constituted in 1807, by the Rev. James Vance, with about twelve or fifteen members. When the Charlestown church was organized, in 1812, the Palmyra church had become almost extinct, and the few remaining members were embodied in the Charlestown church. The Charlestown church was thus the third church organized in Indiana. The fourth was that of Washington, Daviess county, with seventeen members, in 1814. The fifth, that of Madison, with fifteen or twenty members, in 1815. The sixth, that of Salem, in Washington county, in 1816. The seventh, that of Blue River, in Washington county, with seven members, in 1816. The eighth, that of Pisgah, in Clarke county, with fifteen members, in 1816. The ninth, that of Graham, in Jennings county, with seventeen members, in 1817. The tenth, that of New Albany, with ten members, in 1817. The eleventh, that of Hopewell, in Sullivan county, in 1817. The twelfth, that of Jeffersonville in Jefferson county, with fourteen members, in 1818. The thirteenth, that of New Lexington, Scott county, with twenty members, in 1818. The fourteenth, that of Corydon, with seven members, in 1819. The fifteenth, that of Carlisle, in Sullivan county, with nine members, in 1819.

The church at Bloomington was the sixteenth Presbyterian church organized in the new and growing State. It consisted at its organization, of nine persons, Henry Kirkham, Mary Kirkham, Dr. David H. Maxwell, Mary Dunn Maxwell, John Ketcham, Elizabeth Ketcham, Elizabeth Anderson, Elizabeth Lucus and Patsy Baugh. Of these persons, Dr. David H. Maxwell and John Ketcham were, during their lives, prominent and influential citizens. They both took an active part in the Indian war that begun with the battle of Tippecanoe. Their families were obliged to seek shelter in forts. Ketcham's fort, in Jackson county, the region of country in which he had first settled when he came from Kentucky into Indiana, was considered far out from the settlements, and greatly exposed to the savages. The fort itself was never attacked by the Indians, though invested one night by a party, who succeeded in driving off the horses belonging to those in the fort. Ketcham and a comrade, on an errand to a neighboring farm, were waylaid by the Indians, and Ketcham received two severe gun-shot wounds, and his comrade was killed. In a scouting party under Gen. Bartholemew, he is again in imminent peril. Again a comrade falls at his side, fatally wounded, and he escapes only by being quicker with the fatal aim of his rifle than the savage foe, who has singled him out for his victim.

It was in April, 1818, that John Ketcham moved to Monroe county. He built the first mill that was built in the county. The meal his family used while the mill was built, was prepared by a hand mill, the only kind at the time in the county. He was, in time, honored with a Colonelcy of the State Militia, because of the reputation he had gained in the Indian war. He became an associate Judge, and served several times as Representative in the Legislature. He died February 7th, 1865, at the age of eighty-three.

Dr. David H. Maxwell, moved to Bloomington in the spring of 1819. He was much in public life. He was a member from Jefferson county of the Convention of 1816, which framed the constitution with which Indiana, in December, 1816, was admitted as a State into the Federal Union. He was the mover in the convention of the clause in the constitution, which prohibited Slavery, for the introduction of which, into the new State, as shown in Dillon's History of Indiana, strong and persistent efforts had been made. Dr. Maxwell frequently represented the county of Monroe in the Legislature, and was the eighth Speaker of the House of Representatives. He was for twenty-five years a member of the Board of Trustees of the State University, and almost constantly the President of that Board. He was elected an elder of the church in June, 1823, and served the church as such until his death in May, 1854, at the age of sixty-eight.

Of the original members of the church of Bloomington, two still survive, Mrs. Mary Dunn Maxwell, the widow of Dr. D. H. Maxwell, and Mrs. Elizabeth Ketcham, the widdow of Col. John Ketcham. Mrs. Maxwell was born in March, 1788, one year before the adoption of the Federal Constitution. Mrs. Ketcham was born in Rockingham county, Virginia, November 27th, 1781, six weeks after the surrender of Cornwallis at Yorktown. Uniting with the church when about twenty years of age, she has been a member of the church militant for seventy-five years, and in faith and hope, is waiting for her admission into the church triumphant.*

The church at Bloomington was organized in the Court House, a log building erected for temporary use, and of which a pen photograph remains in the contract for its erection, now to be found in the records of the county. It was, according to the terms of the contract, to be built after the manner of double cabins, the first ten feet square, and the second, twelve by twenty, built ten feet apart, with an entry between. It was to be ten feet high, of round logs, all to be neatly butted, then hewed inside and out; the whole to be covered under one roof with four courses of boards on each side; the floors to be out of half timber, well hewed and jointed, and two and a half inches thick when they lay on the sleepers; one door (doorway) in each apartment of said house, with one window in the largest, the doors to be fronting the entry, and shutters made to all and hung on good wooden hinges, the house to be chinked with short blocks, after the manner with stone, and well daubed inside and out and made smooth.

The dwellings of Bloomington were in harmony with its court house. They were log cabins, and dense forests occupied most of its streets and lots. In this same year Fort Wayne was vacated by the United States Government as a frontier military post, and it was left a small trading post for bartering with the Indians for their peltries, the same purpose for which it had been first occupied by the French more than a hundred years before.

In 1810, the population of the Territory of Indiana was

---

* Mrs. Ketcham, since the above was written, has entered into rest, departing this life on Sabbath morning, July 9th. 1876.

24,520. But the streams of immigration were beginning to flow in rapidly upon the new country, and a committee had been appointed by the Legislative Council to locate a permanent Capital for the State. This Council also petitioned Congress for permission to locate a certain quantity of the public lands "lying on the main fork of White River," for this permanent seat of government. The war with the Indians hindered the consummation of this work begun by the Legislative Council. In the enabling act of Congress for the organization of the State, four sections of unsold land were donated for a permanent Capital. In January, 1820, a committee was appointed by the legislature to fix the location of the State Capital. They located it in June of the same year. On the 6th of January, 1821, the Legislature confirmed the action of their commissioners, and on motion of Judge Jeremiah Sullivan, of Madison, afterwards, if not at the time, an elder of the Presbyterian church, the newly established Capital received its name, Indianapolis. In the spring of the same year, 1821, in which the Capital was located, the man, who but two years before was the first settler in the vicinity of Indianapolis, was murdered by the Indians upon the place upon which he had settled, and the horses he had owned were driven off by them.

In the course of a few months after the location of the Capital, a population of some hundreds gathered upon the site of the future city. For this population, flour and meal were packed on horses through a pathless wilderness from the White Water settlement at Connersville, a distance of sixty miles. This was necessary for several reasons. The season was an exceedingly wet one, and malignant fever and ague so prostrated the inhabitants of the new settlement, that they were unable to tend the corn which had been planted, and which choked by the rank growth of weeds, had brought no fruit to perfection. Indianapolis was not destined to a rapid growth in its early days. George Stephenson had not yet succeeded in securing the device for rapid travelling by railway, though working very earnestly and hopefully for it. Indianapolis, before the days of railroads, was too inaccessible a point for rapid growth. The first sale of city lots occurred in October, 1821. In 1831, three-fourths of the town site and donation of the government remained unsold. Among the names of the first arrivals of citizens after the location of the Capital of the State, are the names of Dr Isaac Coe, Caleb Scudder, James Blake and James M. Ray, names that will ever be held in honored remembrance in the history of the Presbyterian church in Indianapolis.

It is a matter of record, that the Rev. Ludlow G. Gaines, of Ohio, a missionary of the General Assembly, preached in a grove upon the site of Indianapolis, several months before the lots now covered by the city had been offered for sale. The first settlers of the new city had the gospel preached to them only when some travelling minister, overtaken by the Sabbath, paused in his journey. This lack of gospel privilege, it is said, was rapidly tending to obliterate the distinction between the Sabbath and other days. One among the settlers became deeply engaged in finding means to arrest the growing desecration. This was Dr. Isaac Coe. His first effort was to organize a Bible class of Christian people. This class first met February 20th, 1822. A Sabbath school was organized April 6th, 1823. It was advertised in the Indianapolis Gazette, as the Indianapolis Sabbath School. So it was for five years, *the* Indianapolis Sabbath School, the only one. It was organized with thirty scholars, its numbers increasing during the year to ninety-eight, with an average attendance of forty. James M. Ray was its first Superintendent, although he was not yet a member of the church. Likewise, James Blake, an active co-laborer in the Sabbath School, and in all the outward work of the church, was not yet a member of the church. It was in a revival in 1830, that these men became by profession of their faith, members of the church.

The Rev. David C. Proctor, a missionary under the direction of the Connecticut Missionary Society, entered the State late in the fall of 1821. In the fall of 1822, although there was yet no church organization at Indianapolis, arrangements were made with him to preach three-fourths of his time at Indianapolis, while every fourth Sabbath he preached to the little church at Bloomington. Thus the way was prepared for the organization of the Presbyterian church at Indianapolis. The church was organized July 5th, 1823, in Caleb Scudder's cabinet shop, the same place in which the Sabbath School had been organized. The Rev. Isaac Reed, who in the fall of 1822 had moved to Owen county, writes in his Christian Traveller:

"My first visit to Indianapolis was through many perils of waters by the way, in company with Mr. Proctor, the 3d of July. On the afternoon of the 4th, I preached to the Presbyterian friends at a cabinet maker's shop; and at the same place, on the morning of the 5th, I preached as moderator in the formation of the church of Indianapolis. The same day two other ministers arrived. The next day was the Sabbath, and there were four ministers with this new formed church. The church was organized with fifteen members. Dr. Isaac Coe and Caleb Scudder were elected elders. A church edifice had been begun in May before the organization of the church, and was so far completed that it was occupied at the sacrament of the Lord's Supper on the Sabbath, the next day after the organization of the church."

The building committee that carried through 'the erection of this edifice, were Dr. Isaac Coe, James Blake, and Daniel Yandes. This church building was thirty-four feet by fifty-four. Its cost was fifteen hundred dollars. The cost of the lot was one hundred dollars.

CHRONOLOGICAL COMPARISONS.

This church building was erected on the frontiers. Only a hundred years before this the foundations of the first Presbyterian church building in the city of New York had been laid, a building sixty by eighty feet, on Wall street, near Broadway, and although contributions for the building were solicited and obtained in Connecticut and Massachusetts, from the infant church in Philadelphia, and also from Scotland, yet for twenty years the church struggled on in poverty, assembling in a house without galleries, six out of its eight windows being closed with boards, poverty preventing their being glazed, and the fraction of light being enough for the handful of people.* The churches of Cincinnati and Louisville had been organized sometime before the church at Indianapolis. Cincinnati had been laid out in 1789, its first Presbyterian church organized in 1790, and its first Presbyterian church edifice erected in 1792. Louisville had been laid out still earlier. In 1780 the legislature of Virginia passed "An act for the establishing the town of Louisville, at the falls of the Ohio," naming the town in honor of Louis XVI., whose troops were then aiding

* Webster's History of the Presbyterian Church, pp. 120, 329.

the Americans in the war of Independence. The first Presbyterian church in Louisville was organized in 1816, and its first church edifice erected in 1816. At the time of the organization of the Presbyterian church at Indianapolis, the Rev. Gideon Blackburn had just been settled as pastor over the Presbyterian church at Louisville. In the spring of 1823, the presbytery of Louisville reported to the General Assembly eleven ministers, thirty-five churches, and nine hundred and ten church members. Of these thirty-five churches, twenty-four were in Indiana, the church of Indianapolis being the twenty-sixth organization of that large portion of the State, which was included within the bounds of the presbytery of Louisville.

At this time, July, 1823, the Presbyterian church at St. Louis was still without a church edifice. A Presbyterian church, consisting of nine members, had been organized by the Rev. Salmon Giddings in St. Louis in November, 1817. A brick church building, forty by sixty feet, was commenced in 1823, but was not finished and dedicated until June, 1825. Its cost was eight thousand dollars. The debt upon it, it is said, was reduced in 1826, by contributions and proceeds of sale of pews, to five thousand dollars.* In Detroit, on the 5th of August, 1816, an informal organization of citizens of Protestant faith was effected by Rev. John Monteith, a missionary of the General Assembly of the Presbyterian church. In 1819, a church edifice was erected at a cost of seven thousand dollars, more than eleven hundred having been obtained by the solicitation abroad of funds. In January, 1825, the church, consisting of forty-nine members, was reorganized, adopting Articles of Faith,

---

* Sprague's Annals, Vol. IV, p. 507.

which fully committed the society to the Presbyterian doctrines and form of government.*

It was not until ten years after the organization of the church of Indianapolis, (in June,) 1833, that the first Presbyterian church of Chicago was organized, with twenty-five members; sixteen of these members of the garrison of Fort Dearborn, and nine citizens of the new city which had been laid out three years before. The Rev. Jeremiah Porter, who came with troops from Green Bay to Chicago in May, 1833, organized the church. Its first edifice for worship was a frame, twenty-six by forty, and was opened for worship January 1st, 1834.

* Manual of First Presbyterian Church of Detroit.

CHAPTER II.

Louisville and Salem Presbyteries—Indianapolis as a Missionary Field—First Ordination in the State—Ordination and Installation at Bloomington—Organization of Churches at Columbus, Franklin, Greencastle and Greenwood—Presbytery of Wabash—Synod of Indiana—Difficulties with Mr. Bush—Presbytery of Crawfordsville—Difficulties in Presbytery—Difficulties Allayed.

1823—1830.

IN 1815, upon petition of the Synod of Ohio, the General Assembly made the Ohio river the dividing line between the synods of Ohio and Kentucky. This placed Indiana Territory within the boundaries of Miami presbytery. In 1817, upon petition of the Louisville Presbytery, it was granted by the General Assembly that so much of the Synod of Ohio as was west of a line drawn due north from the mouth of Kentucky river, should be attached to the Synod of Kentucky. In October, 1823, the Synod of Kentucky constituted all that part of its territory lying within the boundaries of the State of Indiana into a new presbytery, denominated the Salem Presbytery. In October, 1824, the synod added to this presbytery all that part of the State of Illinois which is north of a line running due west from the mouth of White river. At the same time, that part of the State which lies south and west of a line beginning at the mouth of Green river, running due north twenty miles, thence north-westward to the mouth of White river, was attached to the Presbytery of Muhlenburg.

INDIANAPOLIS AS A MISSIONARY FIELD.

In the fall of 1823, the Rev. D. C. Proctor removed to Kentucky. "From this time," writes the Rev. Isaac Reed, then preaching to the Bethany church, in Owen county, "the particular care of the church of Bloomington and of Indianapolis fell upon me, and neither sacraments nor baptism were administered in either except by my ministry, until the arrival of Rev. Mr. Bush, at the latter place, in the summer of 1824, and of Mr. Hall at Bloomington, near the same time." *

While Mr. Reed was thus, through the latter part of 1823 and the first half of 1824, supplying the church at Indianapolis, he wrote thus of it to the United Domestic Missionary Society, a society which in 1826 became merged with the American Home Missionary Society: "Indianapolis, the new and permanent seat of government for the State, is a place of great need and high hope for a *located* missionary. I was lately there, and the session of the church showed me a written resolution of their society, which they design to forward to you. This resolution requests the location of a missionary there. I encouraged them to forward it. There are many reasons why this location should be made. A church is commenced there, which has eighteen members, four of them are male persons. A meeting-house is built, at least raised and covered in. The congregation is willing to raise for your missionary two hundred dollars a year. There is a little Baptist church and a little Methodist society; and there is no church of our order near enough to unite with these to obtain a minis-

---

*Christian Traveller, p. 145.

ter; the nearest is fifty-two miles. It is thought by the session, if they can have a missionary for one year, they can support him after that time, they have such prospects from those who are expected to move there within a year. Now they look to you, brethren, to appoint them one; and he ought to be there as soon as possible. They want a man of such talents as are favorable to collecting and embodying society; one who would be willing to become settled. He should appropriate his Sabbaths to the town, and have week day appointments all about that part of the country."* This communication of Mr. Reed to the United Domestic Missionary Society was published in their report for 1825.

In March, 1824, the session of the church at Indianapolis wrote to Mr. George Bush, a licentiate of the Presbytery of New Brunswick, to secure his services as their minister. Mr. Bush came to Indianapolis July 9, 1824, as a missionary of the Assembly. September 18, 1824, he was called to the pastorate of the church upon a salary of three hundred dollars, and as much more as they could raise.

In January, 1825, the legislature met at the new capital for the first time. The State offices had been transferred from Corydon to Indianapolis in the November preceding.

FIRST ORDINATION IN THE STATE.

On the 4th of March, 1825, a called meeting of the Presbytery of Salem was held in Indianapolis. At this meeting of the presbytery Mr. Bush was received, and also Mr. Baynard Rush Hall, a licentiate of the Presbytery of Philadelphia. The next day Mr. Bush was ordained and installed as pastor of the Presbyterian

---

*Christian Traveller, p. 165.

church of Indianapolis. This was the first ordination of a Presbyterian minister in the State. The church building being still unfinished, the ordination and installation took place in the building that was used for the State capitol, a large brick court house. The Rev. John F. Crowe preached the ordination sermon. The Rev. John M. Dickey presided and gave the charge to the pastor, and the Moderator of Presbytery, the Rev. Isaac Reed, gave the charge to the people.

ORDINATION AND INSTALLATION AT BLOOMINGTON.

At an adjourned meeting of the presbytery at Bloomington on the 12th of the following April, Baynard R. Hall, who had charge of the State Seminary at Bloomington, was ordained and installed pastor of the church at Bloomington. As the church at Bloomington had no edifice, the ordination and installation services took place in the State Seminary building. The Rev. Isaac Reed preached the ordination sermon. The Rev. W. W. Martin presided and gave the charge to the pastor; and the Rev. John M. Dickey gave the charge to the people. The sermon was from II Corinthians 5: 18. "And hath given to us the ministry of reconciliation." The sermon was published.

The church at Bloomington, besides having had Mr. Proctor to preach for them one-fourth of his time during one year, had had previous to that occasional missionary supplies. Among these had been W. W. Martin, from Livonia, Francis McFarland, a missionary of the Assembly, and Archibald Cameron, of Shelbyville, Kentucky. In the fall of 1822, the Rev. C. C. Beattie, now of Steubenville, Ohio, then laboring in the Wabash valley as a missionary of the Assembly's Board of Missions, preached in Bloomington, also in the spring of 1823.

At the time of Mr. Hall's settlement the church had increased to a membership of thirty. A Sabbath school was organized in 1823, and has been held every Sabbath morning since.

COLUMBUS.

The third church organized within the present limits of the Presbytery of Indianapolis, was the church at Columbus. This was organized by Rev. John M. Dickey, July 3, 1824. It consisted of eighteen members. Mr. Joseph Hart was the first ruling elder. Bartholomew county had been organized in 1821, and Columbus was laid out and made the county seat the same year. In 1824, the population of the county was 2,690. The population of Marion county at this time was about the same. That of Monroe county at the same time was 3,400.

The church of Columbus, it is said,* existed many years before it had any settled pastor, or even regular preaching. Mr. Dickey, who organized it, supplied it at an early day, one Sabbath a month for six months. For many years, once each year, he held meetings for several days, including the Sabbath, baptized children, received members to the church, and administered the communion.

FRANKLIN.

November 30th, 1824, the church of Franklin, Johnson county, was organized by Rev. John M. Dickey. The church was constituted with the following five members: George King, Joseph Young, David W. McCaslin, Elenor King and Nancy Young. George King and David W. McCaslin, were chosen elders, and after a sermon by the Rev. George Bush, they were or-

* Historical Discourse of Rev. N. S. Dickey.

dained to the office of ruling elder. The session then received Jane McCaslin, a member of the church on examination.

Johnson county was organized in 1822. The population of the county in 1824 was 910. The Franklin church was the fourth church organized within the present boundaries of the Presbytery of Indianapolis.

GREENCASTLE.

The church at Greencastle, the county seat of Putnam county, was organized with twelve members, by the Rev. Isaac Reed, August 12th, 1825. Putnam county was organized the last day of the year, 1821. In 1824, it had a population of 1,700. Yet, in 1825, from Greencastle west, along one of the main routes to Illinois, there was a stretch of dense forest unbroken for seventeen miles, save by one hut and its adjacent clearing. "To form this church," writes Mr. Reed, "required much previous labor in preaching, visiting and traveling."

GREENWOOD.

On the last day of the year 1825, the Rev. Isaac Reed organized another church in Johnson county. It was the Greenwood church, then called Greenfield. It was organized with nine members. The formation of the church was effected just two years and three months after the arrival of the first two families in the settlement. The day after this church was organized was both New Year's day and Sabbath day. A sermon was preached, which was afterwards published with this title: "The Foundation Stone," 1 Cor. iii: 2. The sermon, when printed, was dedicated to the Rev. Thomas Cleland, D. D., of Kentucky, in these words:

Every member, sir, of the Greenfield church, has come from your bounds, and has been a worshipper in one or the other of your con gregations. This fact, together with my long acquaintance with and friendship for you, as a man, a christian, a gospel minister, and your pen having so often and so ably moved in defence of that fundamental doctrine, which is the subject of the sermon, are my apology for using your name in this dedication.

[Signed,] ISAAC REED.
COTTAGE OF PEACE, FEBRUARY 3D, 1826.

The Rev. George Bush, as commissioner from Salem Presbytery, was a member of the General Assembly of 1825, the first representative from Indiana in that body.

WABASH PRESBYTERY.

By an act of the Synod of Kentucky, October 1825, Salem Presbytery was divided, and two presbyteries, Madison and Wabash, formed. The Columbus church fell within the bounds of Madison Presbytery. The Wabash Presbytery consisted at its formation of five ministers: Samuel T. Scott, Isaac Reed, George Bush, Baynard R. Hall and Stephen Bliss. It had under its care nineteen churches. Among these were Blomington, Indianapolis, Franklin and Greencastle.

SYNOD OF INDIANA.

In 1826 the General Assembly constituted the Presbyteries of Missouri, Salem, Wabash and Madison into a synod denominated the Synod of Indiana. This synod met in Vincennes October 18th, 1826. There were present from churches within the bounds of the present Presbytery of Indianapolis, Baynard R. Hall, minister of the church at Bloomington, George Bush, pastor of the church at Indianapolis, and John Orchard, elder from the church at Bloomington.

DIFFICULTIES WITH MR. BUSH.

In December, 1826, Mr. Bush, in a sermon preached in

the church at Indianapolis, attempted to prove at length that the Presbyterian form of church government was not scriptural, but that the scriptural form of church government was more like that of Independency. The elders of the church remonstrated with him. They thought it was inconsistent with his ordination vows. They labored and bore long with him, but Mr. Bush could not change his views, neither could he cease from propagating them. The church therefore felt constrained to apply to presbytery for a dissolution of the pastoral relation. This they did in March, 1828. Mr. Bush resisted the application of the church. At an adjourned meeting of the Presbytery of Wabash, held in Indianapolis, June, 1828, the request of the church was granted, and the pastoral relation was dissolved. Mr. Bush appealed from the decision of the presbytery to synod. A portion of the church and congregation sympathized with him, and to these he preached at the court house. The synod affirmed the decision of the presbytery, but with resolutions breathing the spirit of fraternal kindness for Mr. Bush, and also blaming in some measure the church. The church carried up a complaint to the General Assembly of 1829 against the synod. When the complaint was taken up, "after considerable discussion and mature deliberation, it was resolved that this business be dismissed on account of informality, and that the papers be returned to the respective parties."

The Rev. John R. Moreland, of the presbytery of West Lexington, was called October 27, 1828, to the pastorate of the church of Indianapolis. Before the installation of Mr. Moreland, a new presbytery had been constituted by the synod in October, 1829.

PRESBYTERY OF CRAWFORDSVILLE.

The new presbytery was that of Crawfordsville. The north line of Vigo, Clay, Owen and Monroe counties was the dividing line between the Crawfordsville and Wabash Presbyteries. Samuel Baldridge, John R. Moreland, Samuel H. McNutt, George Bush, James Crawford, James Thompson, Jeremiah Hill and John L. Thompson, were the ministers constituting the new presbytery. Thirteen churches were reported to the General Assembly of 1830 within the presbytery. Indianapolis was included in this presbytery. It was to have met November 25, 1829, at Delphi, Carroll county, but owing to an extraordinary fall of rain, and the swollen and impassable state of the streams, the presbytery failed to meet. The moderator called the presbytery together at Indianapolis, March 25, 1830. At this meeting of presbytery, the Rev. John R. Moreland was installed pastor of the church at Indianapolis. The Rev. James Thompson preached the installation sermon, the Rev. Samuel Baldridge presided and gave the charge to the pastor, and the Rev. S. H. McNutt gave the charge to the people.

DIFFICULTIES.

At this meeting of the presbytery a committee was appointed to examine and give certificates during the intervals of presbytery, to any ministers from other presbyteries who might come within the bounds of Crawfordsville presbytery and seek to labor in any of its churches. An examination by either one of a committee of three, and certificate of approval, seemed to be deemed sufficient guarantee to the churches that they would not be led astray. The Rev. Jeremiah Hill and Elder Cornelius Smock protested against this action of the presbytery. Presbytery also requested the Rev.

W. W. Woods, a member of Union Presbytery, Tennessee, to desist from preaching in the churches of the presbytery, on account of erroneous views, which it was supposed he held.

These, and other things left on record, indicate that differences and divisions were springing up among the brethren and the churches.

The second meeting of the presbytery was with the Coal creek church, in Parke county, September 30, 1830. At this meeting of presbytery the name of George Bush was ordered to be dropped from the roll, he having absented himself from the meetings of presbytery, and informed the presbytery that he had renounced the jurisdiction of the Presbyterian church.*

DIFFICULTIES ALLAYED.

At this second meeting of the Presbytery of Craw-

---

*There doubtless should be added to this record the well known facts of Mr. Bush's future career. He had determined to consecrate his life to literature, and, as the best field for his exertions, made his residence in New York city, and in 1831 he was elected professor of Hebrew and Oriental literature in its University. In 1840 he commenced the publication of his "Notes, Critical and Explanatory," on the Old Testament. Eight volumes were issued, embracing Genesis, Exodus, Leviticus, Joshua, Judges and Numbers. Devoting himself in 1844 to the publication of a monthly magazine, in which he discussed the nature of prophetic symbols, he soon manifested a disposition to recede from the rules of interpretation and opinions commonly received in the Protestant churches. In 1844 Dr. James W. Alexander wrote to Dr. Hall: "Bush is going fast over to the New Jerusalem. In the *Tribune*, he challenges all the world to prove the resurrection. He has a book coming out on the soul. He practices Mesmerism. He told me of a lady, who can read any one's character by feeling a paper on which he has written, and read me a copy of his own character thus deduced. His talk is mild, self-complacent and fascinating. He has a man translating the German account of the famous Clairvoyante of Prevorst. You can imagine nothing of the sort too big for his swallow." What Dr. J. W. Alexander perceived in 1844 did not, however, occur till 1848, when he consented to receive the rite of ordination privately, and it was administered to him privately by Dr. Lewis Beers, an aged clergyman in the New (Jerusalem) Church, at Danby, New York.—[*Index Volume Princeton Review*, p. 121.

fordsville, the action of the presbytery at its first meeting concerning Rev. W. W. Wood was, upon application of the church at Greenwood, reconsidered and reversed, and Mr. Wood received as a member of presbytery by letter from the Presbytery of West Union.

At an adjourned meeting of presbytery, held in October, 1830, at Madison, during the session of the synod, the following members were present: Samuel H. McNutt, James Crawford, Jeremiah Hill, W. W. Woods, James Thompson and M. M. Post, ministers, and John Covert and James M. Ray, elders.

The following action was taken:

WHEREAS, Harmony of feeling is especially desirable amongst brethren, in order to secure union of effort, and thus promote each other's usefulness as well as happiness; and,

WHEREAS, There are differences of sentiment existing amongst the brethren composing the General Assembly, which, by common consent, are borne with; therefore,

Resolved, That it is inexpedient for this presbytery to enforce the resolutions adopted at the last spring meeting on the subject of examining ministers, credentials, etc., and that said resolutions be and are hereby rescinded.

With this manifestation of the spirit of peace, there was a manifestation of the spirit of missionary zeal. Every minister of the presbytery was requested to spend ten days of missionary labor, including one Sabbath, in the vacancies somewhere in the presbytery, and report at the next stated meeting.

At this same meeting of presbytery, the Rev. David Monfort, although not present, was received by letter from the Presbytery of Chillicothe. Also, the Rev. M. M. Post, reporting the prospects of organizing a church at Logansport, presbytery advised him to continue his labors if he could be sustained, and organize a church as soon as he deemed it expedient.

CHAPTER III.

Presbytery of Indianapolis—First Statistical Report—The Field and its Occupation in 1830—Decision of Presbytery on Representation, Presbytery resisting division—Complaint against Presbytery—Dissensions from diversity in Doctrine—Items—Hopewell—Industrial · aspects and interests—Southport, Danville, Greencastle, Shiloh, Bethany—The field at the time of the great division of the Church.

1830—1838.

AT the meeting of Synod in Madison, October, 1830, the presbytery of Indianapolis was organized.* The action of synod, as recorded in the Minutes of Synod, was this:

Overture No. 4 was taken up, and the following resolutions were adopted:

Resolved, That Revs. Messrs. John R. Moreland, David Monfort, W. W. Wood, and Jeremiah Hill, of the Presbytery of Crawfordsville, and Revs. Messrs. S. G. Lowry and Wm. Sickels, of the Presbytery of Madison, be and they are hereby constituted a new presbytery, to be known by the name of the Presbytery of Indianapolis, including the counties of Marion, Johnson, Bartholomew, and Decatur, and all the territory lying north of those counties; it being understood that the west line of Hamilton, carried north, shall be the line between the presbyteries of Crawfordsville and Indianapolis; and further

Resolved, That said Presbytery of Indianapolis be directed to hold its first meeting at Greensburg on the first Thursday in April

---

* The first volume of the Records of the Presbytery is lost. Existing records begin October, 1837.

next, at 12 o'clock M., and that the Rev. John R. Moreland be appointed to open the presbytery with a sermon, and preside till a moderator shall be chosen; and in case of his absence, the senior minister present shall perform this duty.

Upon the opposite page is a copy of the statistical report made to the General Assembly of 1831, by the Presbytery of Indianapolis at its meeting at Greensburg. The Rev. Samuel G. Lowry was its first commissioner to the General Assembly, representing the presbytery in the General Assembly of 1831.

At this first meeting of the presbytery the Rev. Eliphalet Kent was received and enrolled.

PRESBYTERY OF INDIANAPOLIS.

Statistical Report made to the General Assembly of 1831, by the Presbytery of Indianapolis.

74. Presbytery of Indianapolis.

MINISTERS AND LICENTIATES.	NAMES OF CHURCHES.	Com. added on examination.	Com. added on certificate.	Total of Communicants.	Total of Baptisms.	Missionary fund raised.	Funds for Commissioners.	Theologi'l Seminary funds raised.	Education funds raised.	Contingent fund of the Assembly.	POST OFFICE ADDRESS.
John R. Moreland, P.	Indianapolis, P.			75	16		$3 31				Indianapolis, Ind.
David Monfort, s. s.	Franklin, s. s.	2	26	118	17		3 00	$10 00			Franklin, Ind.
Samuel G. Lowry, P.	Saud Creek, P.		1	104	12						Greenburg, Ind.
Wm. W. Woods, s. s.	Greenfield, s. s.	28	11	92	11	$8 50	2 50				Greenfield, Ind.
Jeremiah Hill, Miss.	{ Rushville, s. s.		8	36		2 00	75				Rushville, Ind.
Wm. Sickles, s. s.	{ Olive Ridge, s. s.		3								Pleasant Ridge, Ind.
Eliphalet Kent, s. s.	{ New Providence, s. s.										Shelbyville, Ind.
	Batavia, s. s.										
	Columbus, v.										Columbus.
	Washington, v.										Indianapolis, Ind.
	Greensburg, v.			51							Greensburg, Ind.
	Mill Creek, v.										
	Noblesville, v.										Noblesville, Ind.
Total	7	13	30	49	476	56	$10 50	$9 56			

Of the counties included within the present Presbytery of Indianapolis, Monroe continued in Wabash Presbytery, and Putnam, Hendricks and Morgan counties in connection with the Presbytery of Crawfordsville. Brown county was still a part of Monroe, and was not organized until 1836. In 1830, the population of the counties now included in the Presbytery of Indianapolis was thus reported in the United States census:

Monroe	6,577	Hancock	1,436
Putnam	8,262	Johnson	4,019
Hendricks	3,975	Bartholomew	5,476
Morgan	5,593		
Marion	7,192	Total	42,470

In Marion county was the church at Indianapolis. Its membership had been increased from thirty at the time Mr. Moreland came to it, to one hundred by 1830, forty having been received upon examination. At Greenwood, the Rev. W. W. Woods was preaching, the church numbering in 1830 sixty-five.

The church at Franklin had increased by 1830, to eighty-one. In 1829, twenty-one had been received by examination. In 1830, twenty-seven were added by certificate, and three by examination, making the whole number eighty-one. Until November, 1830, those who had ministered to the church at Franklin, had been with the church as missionary supplies, each for a short time only. Those who had thus ministered to the church were Isaac Reed, William Duncan, John F. Moreland, Jeremiah Hill and W. W. Wood. In November, 1830, the Rev. David Monfort " commenced labors as a stated supply or missionary."

The church at Columbus was reported by the Presbytery of Madison to the General Assembly of 1829, as having eighteen members.

The church at Greencastle, left in its feebleness without supplies, and without a house of worship, had become extinct.

In 1829, a church was organized by Rev. Isaac Reed, at Poplar Spring, Putnam county.

In November 1830, a church consisting of ten members was organized by the Rev. Isaac Reed, at Putnamville.

The church at Bloomington, having built a comfortable brick edifice, and entered into it in 1829, was in a prosperous condition, having a membership in 1830, of fifty-eight. The Rev. Baynard R. Hall, who had been installed as pastor of the church, after a pastorate of one year, had asked for a dissolution of the pastoral relation, because of his relations to the State Seminary, of which he was the first Professor. He was released from the pastoral care of the church, but continued its stated supply until 1830.

In 1828 the State Seminary became Indiana College, and the Rev. Andrew Wylie, D. D., was elected its first president. In 1830, he became the stated supply of the church at Bloomington.

In 1830 the Rev. Isaac Reed was also residing at Bloomington, having returned to Indiana from Moriah, New York, where he had been, for a short period, pastor of a Congregational church. He was endeavoring to establish a Female School at Bloomington, while also laboring as a missionary in the abounding destitutions of the rapidly settling country. A bird's-eye view of the field at this time shows then, in a population of more than forty thousand scattered over these counties, seven Presbyterian churches, the strongest containing a hundred members, the weakest ten, and all only a few over three hundred. There is one pastor, J. R. Moreland at Indianapolis, and there are two stated supplies,

W. W. Wood at Greenwood, and David Monfort at Franklin, who are wholly given to the work of the ministry. One of these, David Monfort, the last month but one in the year, has just entered the field. There are three other ministers at Bloomington engaged in the work of education, but giving a part of their time to the work of preaching, the Rev. Andrew Wylie, D. D., President of Indiana College, and Baynard R. Hall, Professor in the College, and Rev. Isaac Reed, who is seeking to establish a school for young ladies, while he also gives himself in part to missionary labors. Thus contemplating the field, we very clearly perceive that the Presbyterians are a feeble folk, yet we have the assurance that they are building in the rock, even the Rock of Ages.

DECISION OF PRESBYTERY ON REPRESENTATION.

In October, 1831, the Synod of Indiana greatly reduced in size, the presbyteries of the States of Illinois and Missouri having been erected by the Assembly of 1831 into the Synod of Illinois, met in Bloomington. At this meeting of Synod the roll of synod shows no changes in the membership of the Presbytery of Indianapolis. During the sessions of synod, a resolution passed by the Presbytery of Indianapolis was brought up by overture before synod. The presbytery in the overture asked an answer to the constitutional questions involved. The following was the resolution:

Resolved, That in this presbytery every church be considered as vacant, and entitled to a representation in presbytery, where a regular pastoral relation has not been formed, according to the book of Discipline in the Presbyterian church.

The overture was not answered until the next meeting of synod at Crawfordsville, when it was answered adversely. The interpretation given by the resolution respecting the representation of churches, has, however, since become the law of the church, having been adopted by both Assemblies before the reunion; by the O. S. Assembly in 1847, and the N. S. Assembly in 1851.*

In the statistical report of the presbytery to the General Assembly of 1832, two new names appear on the roll of ministers, James R. Wheelock, stated supply at Greensburg and Mill Creek, and John Todd.

At the meeting of synod at Crawfordsville, just referred to, in October, 1832, from the records of synod, it appears that S. G. Lowry had been dismissed from the Presbytery of Indianapolis to unite with the Presbytery of Crawfordsville.

October 19, the second day of synod, this record is made in the minutes: " The synod then solemnly paused to record the death of one of their members, the Rev. John R. Moreland, who was taken from this world of trial and suffering on the 15th inst."

Mr. Moreland had, a short time previous to his death, been released from the pastoral charge of the church at Indianapolis.

PRESBYTERY RESISTING DIVISION.

Two matters of importance to the presbytery were brought before synod. One was a petition by the minority of the presbytery to have the presbytery divided. The petition was referred to the committee on bills and overtures, who reported in favor of the petition and recommended the formation of a new presbytery, to be called Union, consisting of the counties of Decatur, Bartholomew, Shelby and Johnson, reserving to John Todd and his congregation, and David Monfort and his congregation, the privilege of remaining connected with the Indianapolis Presbytery.

Moore's Digest, pp. 138-139.

After considerable discussion, the subject was indefinitely postponed.

Mr. Wood then obtained leave to bring in the following resolution:

Resolved, That it is the duty of this synod to furnish the petitioners from Indianapolis Presbytery the information called for in relation to the previous steps required of them by the constitution, in order that the synod may regularly and constitutionally act on the subject of their petition.

The subject was referred by synod to a committee of three, Messrs. Matthews, Williamson and Dunn, to report upon before the rising of synod.

The committee reported the following resolution, which was adopted, viz:

That said members of the minority of Indianapolis Presbytery be directed to bring the request for a division directly before the presbytery, and if the presbytery refuse to concur with them in petitioning the synod for a division, then they may bring up their petition to synod by way of complaint, when the synod will consider it regularly before them.

COMPLAINT AGAINST PRESBYTERY.

Another matter of importance before the synod pertaining to the Presbytery of Indianapolis, was a complaint against the presbytery by Rev. W. W. Woods and Rev. J. R. Wheelock. The complaint was against a standing rule of presbytery, requiring an examination on theology of every minister proposing to connect himself with said presbytery, provided any two members should require it. After the complaint was heard, the synod passed the following resolution, viz:

Resolved, That without censuring the Presbytery of Indianapolis, the complaint be sustained, so far as regards the expediency of the standing rule complained of.

To this resolution Messrs. Williamson, Martin and Hummer entered their dissent.

The next meeting of synod was at Indianapolis, October 10, 1833. No change appears to have occurred in the ministers of presbytery during the year.

DISSENSIONS FROM DIVERSITY IN DOCTRINE.

Among the first items of business before synod was the presentation of a petition to synod by the Rev. John S. Weaver, that synod would attach him to the Presbytery of Indianapolis, as he had been dismissed to said presbytery and had as yet had no opportunity to unite with it. Synod thereupon ordered: "That the Presbytery of Indianapolis be directed to meet to-morrow morning at eight o'clock to afford to Mr. Weaver, and also to Rev. Hilary Patrick, an opportunity to present their certificates for admission into said presbytery."

The record states that Mr. Patrick was from the Synod of South Alabama. It is not stated what the previous ecclesiastical relation of Mr. Weaver was.

An exception was also made to the records of presbytery, that the application of Mr. Weaver to be received into presbytery had been refused without any reasons being assigned for the refusal.

Upon the morning of the second day of synod, the stated clerk of the Presbytery of Indianapolis reported to the synod that, agreeably to the direction of the synod, a meeting of presbytery had been held, and Messrs. Patrick and Weaver received.

The clerk of synod likewise reported that there had been put into his hands an appeal from a decision of Indianapolis Presbytery by Rev. James R. Wheelock, also a complaint signed by other members of the presbytery against such decision.

The case in issue, concerning which this appeal was taken, was remanded by synod to the presbytery for the bringing in of a definitive sentence, and as this defect in the proceedings of presbytery occurred in consequence of a disorderly withdrawal of the friends of Mr. Wheelock from the presbytery, it was directed, as the readiest and most orderly way in the unhappy and difficult case, that Mr. Wheelock reserve the prosecution of his appeal until presbytery had passed a definitive sentence, and that the presbytery meet during the recess of synod and issue the case of Wheelock or refer said case to synod.

The case was referred by presbytery to synod. It occupied the whole of synod for two days. On the morning of the third day a committee was appointed to express the judgment of synod. The committee consisted of Andrew Wylie, J. Thompson, John F. Crowe, B. C. Cressy, ministers, and William Alexander, elder.

The committee made the following report, which was adopted:

"That having taken the subject under their serious consideration, they have agreed to recommend to synod, for their adoption, the following resolutions. viz:

"*Resolved*, That it is well known throughout the bounds of the Presbyterian church, in the United States, that a difference of phraseology and mode of illustration, with regard to the doctrinal points referred to, in the charges referred to by Mr. Hopkins, against the Rev. J. R. Wheelock, has for a long time prevailed in our church, and to a certain degree ought to be tolerated. That in using this liberty of expression, ministers of the gospel ought to be very careful not to vary from the form of sound words contained in the standards of our church, since want of due caution in this respect is calculated to give offence, and to awaken unpleasant and injurious suspicions in the minds of many people. And that it appears from the testimony, that Mr. Wheelock has not, in his public ministrations, been sufficiently guarded in this respect. Nevertheless, the testimony, together with Mr. Wheelock's written confession of faith with regard to the points alluded to, does sufficiently shew that Mr. Wheelock does not hold doctrines essentially variant from our standards.

"In regard to the sixth specification, the synod decide that though Mr. Wheelock is not proved to have uttered a wilful falsehood, his language was highly indecorous and offensive; especially as uttered from the pulpit and on the Lord's day.

"As it respects the prosecutor, the synod are of opinion that there is no evidence or reason to believe that he was actuated, in exhibiting charges against Mr. Wheelock, by any other motives than such as become him and all other officers and members of the Presbyterian church, who are solemnly bound to be watchful of its purity and peace; yet he appears not to have taken such previous steps in the case as the spirit of the standard of Discipline requires. Therefore, in view of the whole case, it is further

"*Resolved*, That Mr. Wheelock be solemnly and affectionately admonished, and he is hereby admonished, in his future public ministrations, that he give 'good heed,' and seek to 'find out good and acceptable words;' and further, that the prosecutor and all other members of our church should be admonished to observe the rules prescribed in the Word of God and the standards of our church, respecting commencing process against a gospel minister."

From the foregoing decision the following dissent was presented, and ordered to be entered on the minutes, viz:

"The undersigned dissent from the decision of the synod, by which they declare that 'testimony, together with Mr. Wheelock's written confession of faith, in regard to the points alluded to, does not sufficiently shew that Mr. Wheelock does not hold doctrines essentially variant from those of our standards,' inasmuch as they do firmly believe that the testimony adduced clearly shewed that on the subjects of Federal representation, imputation, and the atonement of Christ, Mr. Wheelock does vary materially from the standards of our church; and moreover, this testimony was abundantly confirmed by Mr. Wheelock's written confession.

"ALEXANDER WILLIAMSON,   WM. SICKELS,
"JOHN FINLEY CROWE,   HENDERSON BELL,
"JOHN CAMPBELL,   WILLIAM BEALE,
"JOHN LIST,   DAVID MCCLURE,
"JOHN HENDRICKS,   JOHN S. WEAVER,
"MATTHEW G. WALLACE,   WM. O. ROSS,
"DAVID MONFORT,   JAMES H. THOMPSON."

ITEMS.

At the meeting of the synod at New Albany in 1834, three new names appear upon the roll of the presbytery, Thomas Barr, Samuel Hurd and W. A. Holliday.

In September, 1834, the church at Indianapolis called the Rev. James McKennan, of the Presbytery of Washington, Pennsylvania. He was installed pastor June 16, 1835.

In October, 1835, J. R. Wheelock was received into Crawfordsville Presbytery by letter from the Presbytery of Indianapolis.

From the roll of Synod at Crawfordsville, in 1836, it appears that Wells Bushnell was received into the Presbytery of Indianapolis during the year. David M. Stewart is also reported in the Assembly's minutes as a licentiate of the presbytery. In 1837, Mr. Stewart is reported pastor of the church at Rushville, and David V. Smock is added to the roll of members as pastor of the church at Knightstown. In October, 1837, W. W. Woods is received into Crawfordsville Presbytery by letter from Presbytery of Indianapolis.

HOPEWELL.

Returning now to the history of the cuurches of the presbytery, we find that in May, 1831, the church of Hopewell was, by order of presbytery, organized with forty members from the Franklin church. In October, 1831, the Rev. D. Monfort was installed pastor of the Franklin and Hopewell churches, upon a salary of three hundred dollars. In explanation of this meagre salary, Judge Banta, in his Historical Address at the Semi-centenary Anniversary of the Franklin church, makes some statements which are of general interest, as giving to us a picture not only of the industrial aspects and economies or household management of Johnson county, but of this entire interior region of country, with its base of supsplies upon the Ohio river, and the farmers, with their teams loaded with the produce of their farms for the exchange of merchandise, threading their way at suitable seasons to the distant river towns. The Judge says: "The people were still without a market in which to sell their surplus produce nearer than Madison, on the Ohio river, sixty-five miles away. Wheat was worth from twenty-five to thirty-five cents per bushel; corn ten, and oats eight. Good work horses sold at from thirty-five and forty dollars per head, to fifty and sixty; cows, at from five to ten dollars each; while all cotton and imported woolen goods, and groceries of all kinds, cost at least double the present prices. Those in the entire county, who were not compelled to toil for daily bread and raiment, you could have counted off on the fingers of your right hand. The men tilled the soil during the tilling season, and cleared land for themselves or others during the fall and winter seasons, and spent the long winter evenings in making and mending shoes for their families, or other domestic labor; while the women not only looked after the ordinary and daily affairs of the household, but spun flax, carded and spun the wool, and wove linens, flannels and jeans, with which all were clothed."

SOUTHPORT.

The church at Southport was organized March 30th, 1833, by W. W. Woods, with twenty-four members dismissed for the purpose from the church at Greenwood. The church was named New Providence at its organization. Otis Sprague and John S. Sebern were elected elders. Rev. Hilary Patrick labored for the church for a short period. The Rev. John Todd also ministered to the church for several years. Its membership in 1838 was forty-one.

DANVILLE.

The church at Danville, Hendricks county, was organized by S. G. Lowry in December, 1832, with nineteen members. Daniel McAuley, Stephen Mahood and Alexander Morris, were elected elders. Mr. Lowry preached for some months for the church once a month. The church was without any stated ministry until 1835, when Rev. Moody Chase removed to Danville, and took charge of the church. A church edifice was erected in 1837. Its membership at the time was thirty-eight.

GREENCASTLE.

The church at Greencastle was reorganized July 14th, 1833, with fourteen members, by S. G. Lowry. In 1834, W. W. Woods commenced his labors with the church and remained until 1837. In that year J. R. Wheelock took charge of the church and continued with it a year and three months. The church worshipped until 1836 in a log house that had been built by the Methodists. In this year they erected a brick edifice forty by fifty feet. In 1836 the membership was forty-nine, in 1837, it was seventy-five.

PUTNAMVILLE.

The church at Putnamville after its organization in 1830, enjoyed the labors a part of the time for nearly four years of Revs. Jeremiah Hill, James Shields and S. G. Lowry. At a communion season in August, 1831, nineteen persons were received by letter. In less than four years the church had increased to sixty-five. W. W. Woods ministered to the church in connection with his labors at Greencastle. His labors at Putnamville continued for nine years.

BLOOMINGTON.

At Bloomington, the Rev. Ransom Hawley had become stated supply of the church in 1834. Prof. Hall had removed to Bedford, Pennsylvania. Mr. Reed not succeeding in his efforts in building up a female school, had gone to Hanover. A personal difficulty between Dr. Wylie, President of the State College, and John H. Harney, Professor in the college, who was also a member of the church, led to a church trial, which caused no little trouble to the church. The case was widely known in its day, passing through presbytery and synod to the General Assembly, and sent back by the General Assembly, again occupied the time of presbytery and synod with all its details. The alienations and divisions thus originated in the church at Bloomington could not but hinder its prosperity. The membership reported to the Assembly in 1838, was seventy-two.

From the minutes of the General Assembly, we find the Shiloh church first reported in 1836, but without the number of its members. In 1837, its membership is reported as thirty-seven.

The Bethany church is first reported in 1837, with thirty members.

The names of South Marion, Sugar Creek and Eagle Creek are in the minutes of the Assembly for 1832. Eagle Creek has then a membership of twenty-five, in 1836, of only nineteen.

In 1830, the church of Columbus was supplied for a time by the Rev. Hilary Patrick. In 1834, the Rev. Michael A. Remley resided at Columbus, and supplied the church. In 1837, Rev. Windsor A. Smith took charge of the church, and supplied it for two and a half years. But there was yet no church edifice. The number of members reported to the General Assembly in 1838, was thirty-five.

From the minutes of the Assembly for 1837 and 1838, we have the membership of the churches as follows:

Franklin	114	Danville	35
Hopewell	106	Greencastle	75
Indianapolis	172	Putnamville	65
Greenwood	132	Bloomington	72
New Providence	41	Columbus	35
Shiloh	28	Poplar Spring	90
Bethany	30		
Eagle Creek	28	Total	1,042
South Marion	19		

On this field are the following ministers: John Todd, David Monfort, Eliphalet Kent, Wm. Sickels, W. A. Holliday, James W. McKennan, Moody Chase, W. W. Woods, Ransom Hawley, Andrew Wylie, D. D., and W. A. Smith. Of these, Dr. Wylie is President of the State College, and wholly occupied with its duties. Rev. W. A. Holliday is also engaged in teaching.

In this field of the present presbytery, there was, two years later, a population of more than 84,000; by counties as follows:

Marion	16,080	Monroe	10,143
Johnson	9,352	Brown	2,364
Hancock	7,535	Bartholomew	10,042
Hendricks	11,264		
Putnam	16,843	Total	84,364
Morgan	10,741		

In this growing population the Presbyterians are still a feeble folk, and unhappily divided. How will they grow when they are no longer quarreling factions in the same church, but divided into two different bodies, each harmonious with itself? We shall see, if we follow on.

CHAPTER IV.

Action of the Presbytery of Indianapolis in the Great Division of the Church—Action of the Presbytery of Crawfordsville—Greencastle First—Greencastle Second—Putnamville, Poplar Spring, Bainbridge, Carpentersville, Bloomington, Columbus.

1838—1850.

In May, 1838, occurred the division of the General Assembly, by which the Presbyterian Church became divided into two denominations. The division accomplished in Philadelphia in May, 1838, was accomplished in the lower judicatories of the church as they were successively convened. Upon the 31st of July, 1838, the Presbytery of Indianapolis met at Franklin, at the call of the moderator, Eliphalet Kent, for the purpose of attending to any business which the peculiar state of the church at the time, and especially within the bounds of the presbytery, might demand.

We, happily, now have the records of the presbytery.

ACTION OF INDIANAPOLIS PRESBYTERY.

The result of this called meeting was that the presbytery adhered to the O. S. Assembly. Against this action the Rev. Eliphalet Kent, the moderator, the Rev. John Todd and Elder Simon Smock, of New Providence, protested, declaring their belief that the New School Assembly was the true Assembly of the Presbyterian church. The churches of Greenwood, South Marion and Eagle Creek united with these brethren in their adhesion to the New School Assembly.

ACTION OF PRESBYTERY OF CRAWFORDSVILLE.

A few days previous to the action of Indianapolis Presbytery, in regard to the division of the church, the Presbytery of Crawfordsville had been convened to hear the report of their commissioners to the Assembly and take such action as might be deemed necessary. The Crawfordsville Presbytery, by a very large majority, adhered to the New School Assembly; and among the churches adhering to the New School Assembly, were the churches of Danville, Greencastle and Putnamville. The church of Bloomington, within the Vincennes Presbytery, adhered to the O. S. Assembly.

It was a sad thing that irreconcilable differences should divide into two bodies the Presbyterian church, and make it two denominations. But it was doubtless far better that the churches in which such irreconcilable differences existed, should be divided into two denominations, each in harmony with itself, and having fraternal regard for the other, and each gradually eliminating from itself the hindrances to a true and lasting union to be consummated in due time, than to continue in a state of unceasing internal strife, in which there was more of nominal than real union, and in which the zeal and strength of the church were more expended in strife upon its differences than in pushing forward steadily the work of evangelization, in saving the perishing and in gaining from the world still wider provinces for the dominion of the Redeemer. Blessed are our eyes, which have seen the repellant differences eliminated and the reunion consummated. Blessed will be the work of our hands as laboring together in the unity of the spirit, this union, thorough and complete as it is, becomes more and more efficient in accomplishing the work which the Lord has given His church to do.

GREENCASTLE FIRST.

After the division of the Assembly in 1838, the Greencastle church continued with the New School Assembly. At the time of the division, the Rev. J. R. Wheelock was ministering to it. But very soon after this, he withdrew from connection with the Presbyterian church. In the minutes of the Crawfordsville Presbytery (N. S.) there is this record, made in March, 1839:

Resolved, That the name of James R. Wheelock be discontinued on our records, he having left our bounds without a dismission and become connected (as we learn) with another ecclesiastical body.

In the fall of 1840, the Rev. James Shields, who had been previously supplying for several months the church at Greencastle, became its pastor. This relation continued only until 1842. In 1842 an addition was made to the church of fifty-six persons. Rev. Ransom Hawley was stated supply from February, 1843, to the fall of 1845. The church continued to increase in numbers during these years. In December, 1845, Rev. Thomas S. Milligan became stated supply of the church and continued in that relation until 1850. Nineteen were added to the church 1847. The number of members reported to the General Assembly as in connection with the church in 1850 was one hundred and ten.

GREENCASTLE SECOND.

In 1849, the second church of Greencastle was organized in connection with the Presbytery of Crawfordsville, O. S. It was organized by Rev. W. Y. Allen, with thirteen members, some of whom were dismissed by letter from the first church.

PUTNAMVILLE.

On the 26th of November, 1841, the Rev. Ransom Hawley commenced his labors in the church at Putnamville, in connection with the church of Bethany, Owen county, for one-half his time. In 1849, a new house of worship was erected at Putnamville. In 1850, the membership reported to the Assembly was fifty-seven.

POPLAR SPRING, BAINBRIDGE AND CARPENTERSVILLE.

The church of Poplar Spring had been divided in the division of the church. The majority adhered to the New School body. The name of the church was changed in 1843 to Bainbridge. It reported in 1850, a membership of forty-three. The Old School portion of the church were organized into a separate body in 1839. They numbered at the time of organization, seventeen members. This became the Carpentersville church. It reported in 1850, a membership of twenty-seven.

BLOOMINGTON.

The Rev. Ransom Hawley, who, as stated supply took charge of the church at Bloomington in 1834, continued in that relation to the church until the fall of 1841, when he removed to Putnamville. During Mr. Hawley's ministry at Bloomington, eighty-three persons were received into the membership of the church, thirty-seven upon profession, forty-six by letter. At this time the church of Bloomington was receiving aid from the Board Missions to the amount of a hundred and a hundred and fifty dollars a year.

In the spring of 1843, the Rev. W. W. Martin removed from Livonia to Bloomington, and became stated supply of the church. He remained two years, and then returned to Livonia. During these two years, twenty-six persons were added to the church, sixteen by profession of faith, ten by letter. The number of members reported to the Assembly in 1845, was eighty-four. In the report of 1846, this number was reduced to sixty-eight.

Upon the return of Mr. Martin to Livonia, the Rev. Alfred Ryors, Professor in the State University, the college having become the State University in 1839, was invited to supply the pulpit for a year, or until a pastor could be secured. Mr. Ryors accepted the invitation, and ministered to the church for a little more than two years, until July, 1847. These were years of great blessing to the church. The members of the church had a mind to work. They sought and obtained the labors of a colporteur to distribute tracts and religious books among the people. The congregation was divided into districts by the elders, and a personal responsibility for each district laid upon the elder to whose oversight it was entrusted. The spirit of the Lord moved upon the hearts of the people, and one and another was added to the church. For more than a year this spirit of earnest work was manifested by the people. Doubtless with this spirit of work there was a spirit of prayer. In the meantime the Synod of Indiana met with the church in 1846, no doubt strengthening and confirming the church. In the spring of 1847, there was a deepening and growing interest. At this time the minister and session sought for help. Upon the 21st of May, the Rev. Dr. Nathan R. Hall, of Kentucky, came to Bloomington by invitation to assist in a protracted meeting. Dr. Hall preached for ten days, preaching at 9 A. M., having an inquiry and prayer meeting at 3 P. M., and preaching again at 7 P. M., with a meeting for prayer, exhortation and inquiry following. During these meetings thirty-eight persons were received upon profession of their faith. A number were received a short time afterwards.

The number received during Prof. Ryors' ministry was seventy-two, sixty-three upon profession of faith, nine by letter.

In July, 1847, the Rev. Levi Hughes was invited to supply the church for a year. Mr. Hughes had been received into the church of Bloomington upon profession of his faith not quite four years before. He was at that time studying law. His convictions of duty turned him to preparation for the ministry. After he had completed a three years' course of theological study in the Seminaries at New Albany and Princeton, he was invited to become the stated supply of the church at Bloomington. He accepted the invitation, and after this term of service he was called and settled as pastor. This pastorate only continued, however, until the spring of 1851, when Mr. Hughes removed to Logansport, having accepted a call to the first Presbyterian church of that place.

In 1850, the membership of the church at Bloomington as reported to the General Assembly, was one hundred and twelve.

COLUMBUS.

The historical records of the church at Columbus are very meagre. The Rev. B. M. Nyce supplied the church during a term of years between 1840 and 1850. Under his ministry, the first Presbyterian church edifice was erected in Columbus. It was built about the year 1841, mainly as a result of Mr. Nyce's persistent and indomitable energy. The church was then very feeble, and considered itself too poor for such an undertaking, Mr. Nyce himself, aided by a few ladies, solicited subscriptions in material, work and money, and when they could get no more commenced the work and pressed it until the means were exhausted. Then it stood still and the process of procuring means and then expending was again repeated. Thus the work progressed until it was finally completed, without debt, at a cost of about twelve hundred dollars.

Mr. Nyce's labors in building the church, in teaching in the county Seminary, which he did for several years, and his preaching were spoken of in the highest terms by those who knew him and his work. The church paid him a salary of one hundred and seventy-five dollars, all they could raise. Several seasons of religious interest were enjoyed during his ministry. Mr. Nyce left Columbus in 1849. In the fall of 1849, Mr. Charles Merwin was called to supply the pulpit for one year. During this year several were added to the church. The number of members reported to the General Assembly of 1850, was ninety.

CHAPTER V.

Second Church of Indianapolis—Indianapolis Presbytery, N. S.—Enlargement of Presbytery—Ministerial Changes— Changes in Churches—Missionary Work—Pastoral Relation—Report to General Assembly.

1840—1850.

SECOND CHURCH OF INDIANAPOLIS.

ONE of the first important effects within the Presbytery following the great division in the Presbyterian Church, was the formation of the Second Presbyterian church of Indianapolis. This was organized by Rev. James H. Johnson, November 19, 1838, in the Marion county seminary, a small brick building standing, until 1860, at the south-west corner of University Square. The original members of the church were fifteen in number. Their names are as follows: Bethuel F. Morris, Daniel Yandes, Luke Munsell, Lawrence M. Vance, Mary J. Vance, Sidney Bates, William Eckert, Alexander H. Davidson, Robert Mitchell, William S. Hubbard, Joseph F. Holt, Margaret R. Holt, John L. Ketcham, Jane Ketcham and Catherine Merrill. On the 20th of November, the day after the organization, they issued a call to Rev. Sylvester Holmes, of New Bedford, Massachusetts. The call was declined. Some weeks later, January 15, 1839, they invited Rev. John C. Young, of Danville, Kentucky, to become their pastor, but this overture also was unsuccessful. The Rev. Elihu Baldwin, president of Wabash College, was solicited to take charge of the new church. He likewise declined. On the 13th of May, the Rev. Henry Ward Beecher, then of Lawrenceburg, Indiana, was called to the pastorate. He accepted the call, and entered upon his work in the church July 31, 1839. At this time the church had increased to a membership of thirty-two. The county seminary was occupied for one year as a place of worship. The church then went into its own edifice, occupying at first the lecture room. Soon, however, the house was completed, and its dedication occurred October 4, 1840.

INDIANAPOLIS PRESBYTERY, NEW SCHOOL.

A second effect of importance following the division of the Presbyterian church into Old and New School, was the formation of the New School Presbytery of Indianapolis.

The Rev. Eliphalet Kent, and the Rev. John Todd, with the churches within the bounds of Indianapolis Presbytery adhering to the N. S. Assembly, had, in the adherence of the majority of that presbytery to the O. S. Assembly, become connected with the Presbytery of Madison. In October, 1839, the synod of Indiana, N. S., passed the following:

Resolved, That the Presbyteries of Madison and Crawfordsville be divided, and the Presbytery of Indianapolis formed, embracing the following territory, viz: The counties of Morgan, Johnson, Shelby, Rush, Hancock, Henry, Marion, Hendricks, Hamilton and Madison. Said presbytery to meet at Franklin, on the last Thursday of March (1840), at 11 o'clock A. M. The Rev. John Todd, or in his absence the next oldest minister present, shall preach the opening sermon, and preside until another moderator be chosen.

In accordance with the above order of synod, the Presbytery of Indianapolis (N. S.) met at the appointed time at Franklin. The Rev. John Todd having deceased, the sermon was preached by the Rev. Moody Chase. The presbytery was opened with prayer by the moderator *pro tem*. The Rev. Moody Chase was chosen moderator, and Henry Ward Beecher, temporary clerk, and subsequently stated clerk. The members present were: Ministers, A. G. Dunning, Moody Chase and Henry Ward Beecher; elders, Garret Sorter and E. N. H. Adams. Rev. E. Kent, another member, was absent. At an adjourned meeting of the presbytery, held at Indianapolis the next month (April), the Rev. P. S. Cleland was received by letter from the Salem Presbytery. The churches included within the original limits of the presbytery were the following: Danville, Brownsburg, New Winchester, Second Indianapolis, New Providence or Southport, Greenwood, South Marion, afterwards Mt. Pleasant, Eagle Creek, Highland, Sugar Creek and Batavia.

At the meeting of the General Assembly (N. S.) in 1840, the territory in south-east Indiana, which had belonged to the Synod of Cincinnati, was attached to the Synod of Indiana. At the meeting of the synod in October, 1840, so much of the territory added to the synod by the act of the Assembly as was north of Decatur and Ripley counties was added to the Presbytery of Indianapolis.

ENLARGEMENT OF PRESBYTERY.

In October, 1845, the presbytery was enlarged by the following action of synod:

Resolved, That the county of Boone, embracing the Rev. Thompson Bird and the churches of Lebanon, Bethel and Thorntown, be detached from the Presbytery of Crawfordsville and attached to the Presbytery of Indianapolis; and that the county of Decatur, embracing the Rev. Jonathan Cable and the church of Sand Creek, be detached from the Presbytery of Madison and attached to the Presbytery of Indianapolis.

Previous to this enlargement of the presbytery, there was frequent failure of a quorum at appointed times of meeting.

MINISTERIAL CHANGES.

In October, 1841, William N. Stimson, who had been received as a licentiate from the Presbytery of Cincinnati, was ordained as an evangelist at a meeting of the presbytery in Highland church.

At this meeting of presbytery, Rev. Alvah G. Dunning was dismissed to the Presbytery of Cincinnati. Presbytery also appointed Messrs. Cleland and Chase to visit and spend one Sabbath at Noblesville before the next stated meeting Likewise W. N. Stimson and Henry Ward Beecher were to visit and hold communion service with the church at Danville, spending a Sabbath with the church.

In April, 1842, Rev. Moody Chase was dismissed to the Presbytery of Crawfordsville.

Presbytery in session at Danville, April, 1843, received from the Presbytery of Cincinnati and ordained Mr. H. Hanmer, who was ministering as stated supply to the church at Danville. "Mr. Hanmer," writes one of the elders of the church concerning him, "was a young man of talent and piety, and much beloved by his people. Before the close of the first year of his ministry, he became insane and was taken to his home in Connecticut by his friends." In 1859 his name was dropped from the roll.

In August, 1843, presbytery, in session at Indianapolis, licensed Mr. Charles Beecher. In September, 1844, he was dismissed to the care of the Presbytery of Logansport.

In November, 1845, Rev. Benjamin M. Nyce was received from Salem Presbytery. April, 1846, Rev.

James McCoy was received from Logansport Presbytery. Also B. F. Stuart, a licentiate, was received from the Presbytery of Cincinnati and ordained. November, 1847, he was dismissed to Salem.

April, 1847, Rev. Theophilus Lowry was received from the Presbytery of Crawfordsville. He was with the church of Danville until the spring of 1849. In September, 1850, he was dismissed to the Presbytery of Crawfordsville.

In September, 1847, the labors of Henry Ward Beecher in the Second church of Indianapolis closed, and in October a letter of dismission was granted to him by presbytery "to join the body with which the Plymouth church, Brooklyn, New York," was connected. From the beginning of Mr. Beecher's ministry in the Second church there was a gradual and hopeful growth. In the beginning of 1842, a very precious revival was experienced. At three communion seasons, held successively in February, March and April, 1842, nearly one hundred persons were added to the church on profession of their faith. Early in the following year, at the March and April communions, the church had large accessions, as it had also in 1845. During this pastorate of more than eight years, the membership of the church had increased to two hundred and seventy-five.

From September, 1847, to April, 1848, the Second church of Indianapolis was temporarily supplied by Rev. Shubert Granby Spees.

In September, 1848, Rev. Abraham S. Avery, who had been employed by the missionary committee as the missionary of the presbytery, was received from Pataskala Presbytery, Ohio.

Mr. Avery was soon prostrated by sickness, and unable to continue his missionary labors. In his sickness he was not forsaken by his brethren, but received their sympathies and substantial aid, while the funds contributed to missionary purposes were employed in securing, during the summer of 1849, at twenty dollars per month, the labors of Mr. George Davis, a licentiate of the Presbytery of Cincinnati.

October, 1848, Clement E. Babb, a licentiate of the Presbytery of Dayton, was received. A call from the Second church of Indianapolis having been placed in his hands, and having signified his acceptance, he was ordained and installed pastor of the church.

October, 1848, Rev. W. H. Rogers was received from the Presbytery of Cincinnati.

April, 1849, Amos Jones, a licentiate of the Presbytery of Cincinnati, was received. At an adjourned meeting of presbytery in May, he was ordained. He was stated supply of the church at Danville until 1853.

September, 1849, Rev. Sylvanus Warren, of the Presbytery of Athens, Ohio, was received. His labors were connected with the American Tract Society. In September, 1850, he was dismissed to Salem.

Also, in September, 1849, Rev. Benjamin F. Cole, of the Presbytery of Crawfordsville, was received. A call from the churches of Thorntown and Bethel was put into his hands, and, having accepted the call, a committee was appointed to install him. His installation was reported at the next meeting of presbytery.

April, 1850, James McCoy was dismissed to Presbytery of Salem.

CHANGES IN CHURCHES.

In August, 1842, the New Pisgah church was organized.

In September, 1844, the organization of Stoney Creek church was reported to presbytery in session at Noblesville. Also the organization of a church at Edinburgh was reported, and it was further ordered that the members of the church of Batavia, in the neighborhood of Edinburg, be enrolled among the members of the church at Edinburg, and the name of the church of Batavia be dropped from the roll.

April 1846, the organization of the church of Andersontown was reported, also of the churches of Pendleton and Upper Sugar Creek. These two last churches, however, seem to have never been fully organized, and they had but a short and sickly existence. April, 1847, the organization of a church at Greenfield, Hancock county, was reported.

September, 1850, the Sand Creek and Clarksburg churches sent a request to the presbytery for permission to unite with the Felicity Presbytery of the Free Presbyterian church. The request was complied with, and the names of these churches dropped from the roll.

MISSIONARY COMMITTEE.

April, 1848, Rev. J. Cable, Rev. E. Kent and Dr. W. H. Wishard, were appointed a committee to employ a missionary. A co-operating committee of one from each church in the presbytery was appointed to raise funds for the support of the missionary. This missionary committee was more than a nominal one. It succeeded in accomplishing missionary work.

REPORT OF HOME MISSIONARY COMMITTEE.

September, 1849, the Committee on Home Missions made the following report, which was adopted:

"The survey of our field of labor awakens painful feelings. So much territory lying waste, nominally under our care yet never represented at our meetings. Your committee recommend a more systematic effort to meet the wants of the perishing souls, which Providence has crowded around us. And to secure this object, they suggest, that presbytery elect annually a Board on vacancies, supplies and destitutions, to consist of two ministers and one elder, which shall meet as often as once in two months, and may meet oftener in case of special business. That this Board be instructed to secure men for our vacant churches and destitute territory as fast as possible. That this Board have no power to pledge the presbytery for money without a special vote, but that the presbytery recommend them and their work to all our churches, and will voluntarily aid them in raising funds for such objects as they present. That the churches that have no stated preaching be directed to apply to the Board between the meetings of presbytery for supplies, and that the Board secure members of presbytery to visit those places occasionally.

COMMITTEE ON PASTORAL RELATION.

The presbytery, with its increasing strength, and girding itself for presbyterial mission work, took also the following action respecting the pastoral relation :

Presbytery believes that it is the policy and interest of the Presbyterian church, and that it would be for the glory of God and the good of the community at large, to establish a permanent relation between the preachers and the people, according to our excellent form of government, Chapters 15 and 16, which provides for and enjoins the settling of a pastor over every church, when it shall be practicable. That for the want of such permanent relation, the churches are suffering, not only the want of the stated means of grace, but all the interests of the church are languishing. Seminaries and schools, Sabbath schools, Tract distribution, Missionary operations, and all the means of building up an intelligent church and evangelizing the world, are entirely wanting or are in a languishing condition. Therefore

Resolved, 1st, That we advise every church to secure a permanent pastor as speedily as possible.

Resolved, 2d, That this presbytery will not, unless for very peculiar reasons, agree to grant the relation of stated supply between a minister and church longer than one year.

REPORT OF COMMITTEE ON PASTORAL RELATION.

September, 1849, the Committee on the Pastoral Relation made the following report :

That the churches of Greenwood, New Providence and South Marion have been enjoying the labors of Brother Cleland for many years without installing him pastor, and they recommend that presbytery appoint a committee to meet those churches and confer with them on the subject between this and the first day of December, and secure, if they can, a compliance with the rule of presbytery on the subject.

Messrs. Babb and McCoy, were appointed a committee as above recommended.

As the result of this action, a call for the pastoral services of P. S. Cleland was made by the churches to which he had been so long ministering, and in May, 1850, he was installed by a committee of presbytery. The pastorate was happy and endured for many years.

REPORT OF 1850 TO GENERAL ASSEMBLY.

The Presbytery reported to the Assembly of 1850, thirteen ministers, twenty-one churches and eight hundred and twenty-one members. Of these churches, ten, containing six hundred and twenty-five members, were within the boundaries of the present Presbytery of Indianapolis.

CHAPTER VI.

Presbytery of Indianapolis, O. S.—Churches Organized—Ministerial Changes—Lessons from the History of Franklin Church—Ministerial Support—Missionary Work—Organization of Whitewater Presbytery, and Changes in the Boundaries of the Presbytery.

1838—1850.

PRESBYTERY OF INDIANAPOLIS, OLD SCHOOL.

We turn now to the Presbytery of Indianapolis, Old School.

In the fall of 1838, the pastoral relation between the church of Hopewell and Rev. D. Monfort was dissolved, that Mr. Monfort might give his undivided labors to the church at Franklin. Application was made through the presbytery to the Board of Missions for aid to the amount of two hundred dollars. The salary was five hundred. The presbytery returned the application to the church with directions that they make a vigorous effort to increase the amount subscribed for their pastor's support. This vigorous effort resulted in cutting down the application to the Board of Missions to one hundred and fifty dollars.

CHURCHES ORGANIZED.

May 18th, 1838, Rev. David V. Smock organized a church at Greenfield, styled Hancock church. Wm. T. Templeton, an elder from said church, was admitted to a seat in presbytery. Supplies were appointed for several successive years for this church. A new church was organized in connection with the New School Presbytery in the spring of 1847.

September, 1839, the organization of a church at Andersontown was reported to presbytery. Rev. Robert Irwin was appointed to supply it one Sabbath. In June, 1846, the name of this church was dropped from the roll. In 1846, the organization of a church at Andersontown was reported to the New School Presbytery.

The Presbytery of Oxford having organized the churches of Muncietown and Stony Creek, supposing said churches to be within their territory, and having reported these facts to the Presbytery of Indianapolis, these churches were taken under the care and placed upon the roll of presbytery in 1839.

The organization of the following churches is reported in successive years:

New Burlington, April, 1841.
Middletown, April, 1842.
Union, Decatur county, April, 1843.
Amity, Hamilton county, April, 1844.
Windsor, Randolph county, April, 1844.
Newcastle, April, 1844.
Yorktown, September, 1845.
Concord, Rush county, September, 1845.
Georgetown, Brown county, December, 1845.
Napoleon, September, 1846.
Harmony, Bartholomew county, April, 1848.
New Prospect, Johnson county, September, 1850.

MINISTERIAL CHANGES.

Mr. Joseph G. Monfort was received October 1838, as a licentiate from the Presbytery of Oxford. He became supply of the Greensburg and Sand Creek churches for six months, giving to each church one half his time. April, 1839, he was ordained and installed pastor of these congregations. October, 1842, he was released from the pastoral care of these churches to prosecute an agency for the endowment of the Theological Seminary at New Albany. May, 1845, he was again installed pastor of the church at Greensburg.

W. G. Holliday was dismissed to Crawfordsville Presbytery, October, 1838.

April, 1839, Rev. Robert Irwin and Rev. Michael Carpenter were received from the Presbytery of Oxford.

Rev. Robert Irwin was supply of the church at Muncietown. He received a call to the church in 1843, for one half of his time, and was installed pastor. The name of the church was changed in 1846, to Muncie.

April, 1839, the pastoral relation between J. W. McKennan and first church at Indianapolis was dissolved. By request of the church, Mr. McKennan was appointed supply of the church until next meeting of presbytery.

September, 1839, a call having been given to Rev. James W. McKennan by the congregation of Cross Roads, Washington Presbytery, and he having stated his acceptance of the call, it was ordered "that he be furnished with the proper testimonials and be required to repair to the Presbytery of Washington, that the proper steps may be taken for his regular settlement."

September, 1839, Wm. Sickles became supply of Shiloh for one half of his time. April, 1843, he was dismissed to the Presbytery of Oxford, again received from Oxford September, 1844, and in June, 1846, dismissed to the Presbytery of Madison.

April, 1839, J. S. Weaver was dismissed to the Presbytery of Oxford.

April, 1840, Rev. Sayrs Gazely was received from the Presbytery of Cincinnati, a call having been presented to him by the church of Hopewell. Having accepted it, he was installed the third Saturday of May, by W. Sickles and D. Monfort, a committee of presbytery. In April, 1842, this pastoral relation was dissolved.

November, 1840, Mr. Colvin McKinney, a licentiate of Oxford Presbytery, was received, and it being deemed necessary that he should be invested with full ministerial power in the churches of Shelbyville and St. Omar in which he was laboring, he was ordained as an evangelist. Of his examination we find these records: "Mr. McKinney delivered his sermon, which was not deemed satisfactory, it being partly extemporaneous. Resolved, that Presbytery require of Mr. McKinney a written discourse on the subject assigned as a part of trial without regarding the unwritten sermon preached before us yesterday as any part of trial. Mr. McKinney presented a written sermon on the subject assigned, after which he was further examined on Theology, which sermon and examination were sustained." June, 1843, Mr. McKinney was dismissed to Oxford Presbytery.

In December, 1840, Mr. Phineas D. Gurley, a licentiate of the Presbytery of North River, was received, ordained and installed pastor of the First church at Indianapolis. In June, 1842, the church determined to build a new house of worship. It was occupied in May, 1843, and completed in 1846, at a cost of between eight and nine thousand dollars. In the second year of Mr. Gurley's ministry, forty-two members were received upon profession of their faith. For four successive years the church was increased with goodly numbers on profession of their faith. In November, 1849, the pastoral relation of Mr. Gurley to the church was dissolved. There was received into it during his ministry, two hundred and seventeen persons, one hundred and fifty-eight of these upon profession of their faith, and fifty-nine by letter. The total membership reported to the General Assembly in 1850, was two hundred and six.

In February, 1843, the pastoral relation between D. V. Smock and the church at Knightstown was dissolved. June, 1843, calls from the churches of Hopewell and Shiloh were put by presbytery into his hands. He accepting, was installed by committee of presbytery. This pastoral relation was dissolved in July, 1850.

September, 1845, John Dale, a licentiate of Salem Presbytery, was received, ordained and installed as pastor of the church at Knightstown, for two-thirds of his time. This pastoral relation was dissolved in March, 1850, and in April following, Mr. Dale was dismissed to the Presbytery of Logansport.

August, 1843, George S. Rea, who had previously been received as a licentiate from the Presbytery of Oxford, was ordained and installed as pastor of the church of Ebenezer. This pastoral relation was dissolved April, 1844. Mr. Rea was dismissed September, 1846, to the Presbytery of Iowa.

The Rev. T. A. Hendricks, who had been licensed by the presbytery April, 1841, was ordained and installed pastor of the churches of St. Omar and Shelbyville. This pastoral relation was dissolved April, 1845, on account of ill health of the pastor, disabling him for his work. Mr. Hendricks was dismissed April, 1847, to the Presbytery of Vincennes.

In October, 1846, the Rev. Francis Monfort was received from the Presbytery of Oxford and installed over the churches of St. Omar and Concord.

September, 1847, J. M. Wampler, a licentiate of Oxford Presbytery was received. He ministered to the church of Shelbyville, and was ordained June, 1848.

He was dismissed April, 1849, to the Presbytery of Logansport.

In September, 1844, B. F. Woods, a licentiate of Salem Presbytery, was received. In May, 1845, he was ordained and installed pastor of the Bethany and New Providence churches. This pastoral relation was dissolved April, 1848.

J. C. King, a candidate under the care of the presbytery, was licensed April, 1844. September, 1845, he was ordained and installed pastor of the church of Sand Creek for one-half his time.

D. A. Wallace, a candidate under care of presbytery, was licensed April, 1844. In June, 1847, he was ordained and installed as pastor of the church of Georgetown for one-half his time. This pastoral relation was not of long continuance. Mr. Wallace was dismissed to the Presbytery of White Water July, 1849.

In April, 1844, W. A. Holliday was received from the Presbytery of Oxford. September, 1847, Mr. Holliday's name was dropped from the roll, he having united with the Associate Reformed Church. April, 1849, he was again received from that body.

April, 1848, John Ross was received from Presbytery of Oxford.

September, 1848, D. D. McKee was received from the Presbytery of Alleghany.

July, 1849, Henry I. Coe, a licentiate of the Presbytery of New Brunswick, was received. He was ordained March, 1850.

At the same time, Hugh Marshall was received on probation as a foreign minister from the Presbytery of Armagh, Scotland. A few months afterwards he was dismissed to the Presbytery of Green Brier.

March, 1850, Isaac L. Lyon, a candidate under the care of Albany Presbytery, was received and ordained.

September, 1850, he was dismissed to the Presbytery of Iowa.

July, 1850, James Gallatin was received from the Presbytery of Iowa.

September, 1850, the pastoral relation between Dr. David Monfort and the church of Franklin was dissolved. Dr. Monfort was also granted a letter of dismission to the Presbytery of White Water. Presbytery passed the following resolutions:

> *Resolved*, 1st, That in dismissing Dr. Monfort, for twenty years a father in the presbytery, we can not do justice to our feelings without expressing gratitude to the Head of the church, who has so long spared to us his valuable life, labors and counsels. We shall part with him with sincere regret, and our best wishes and prayers shall follow him to any new sphere to which he may be called.
>
> 2d, That a copy of this minute be sent with the dismission, properly certified.
>
> 3d, That the presbytery sympathize with Dr. Monfort's late charge in their destitution, and hope they may be soon supplied by a regular pastor, and be eminently prospered by the King of Zion.

FRANKLIN.

Judge Banta, in his history of the Franklin church, gives succinct statements of the blessed results of this long pastorate. He also gives illustrations in his narrative of facts of the baleful and blighting results of bitterness, alienations and strifes upon the interests of the church, the salvation of souls, and the glory of Christ. Such teachings from the history of any of our churches ough not to be forgotten.

In the history of the church of Franklin, alluded to, these statements are made: "During the years of Dr. Monfort's preaching here, the record shows that two hundred and seventy-nine in all united with the church, one hundred and forty-nine on profession, and one hundred and forty-eight on certificate. In 1839, from July

21st to 28th, eighteen converts were admitted. From this on to 1842, yearly additions both on certificate and examination were made, but no special manifestation of God's grace appears until January of that year, when from the 5th of that month to the 19th of the month following, thirty-seven were taken into the church on profession. This ingathering brought the membership, at the date of the presbyterial report, made in April of the following year, up to one hundred and eighty-seven. But from thence on to 1851, a period of nine years, there was a slow but sure decline." "Right here," says Judge Banta, "one of the most impressive lessons which the history of this church presents may be learned. During the years which mark the decline of this church under Dr. Monfort's pastorate, a bitter and unrelenting personal warfare was waged between certain of the members. I know nothing of the merits of this controversy; I know not who was right and who was wrong. But for an examination of the records, I would not have known of any difficulty at all, and I therefore censure no man, no party; I only note the fact of the dissension. No doubt during these gloomy years the pastor preached with all the clearness that marked his sermons of former years; no doubt his appeals were as persuasive and his exhortations as eloquent; no doubt sinners felt the arrows of conviction, but the war within the camp went furiously on, and inquirers sought other folds or turned their backs on the church forever. All the actors in that whirl of strife are dead save one. Their bodies have returned to the dust, and their sad difficulties have disappeared with them. The merits of their controversy no one now knows or cares to know. How insignificant it must have been, and yet how baleful in its influence upon the cause of Christianity. Brethren, let us take the lesson to our hearts. Forever let us sink out of sight and memory every element of controversy, every vestige of discord."

SUPPORT OF THE MINISTRY.

From the begining, presbytery was clear and decided in its teachings, and in the use of its authority as to the support of the ministry. In September, 1838, the following overture was presented: Should not every church have one or more deacons regularly elected and ordained, to take care of the poor and manage the pecuniary matters of the church? This was answered in the affirmative, and the churches which had not deacons were directed to have that office filled so soon as practicable.

In April, 1839, the following resolutions are passed:

Resolved, 1st, That presbytery earnestly recommend to the early attention of their churches the minute adopted at the last session of presbytery as to the election and ordination of deacons.

Resolved, 2d, That the special and faithful attention of the deacons be requested to the prompt collection of the pastor's support regularly; and that the members of the churches be earnestly solicited both to subscribe sufficient amounts for the comfortable support of their pastor or supply, and also to make that subscription available for such purpose by its being regularly paid.

At this same meeting of presbytery, the churches were called upon to report settlement with their pastors and supplies. All reported full settlement, except the churches of Franklin and Rushville. These were directed to settle their arrearages, and present the evidence of a settlement with their pastors at the next stated meeting.

The following resolution was also passed:

Resolved, That it be enjoined upon the deacons of our churches to report to presbytery, at its regular meetings, the state of the accounts between congregations and their pastors, the nature and extent of their pecuniary engagements with each other, shewing the exact amounts unsettled, together with the general character of their respective congregations in meeting all congregational engagements. The foregoing is charged as an official duty, which deacons may not neglect.

MISSIONARY LABORS OF PRESBYTERY.

An earnest application was sent to the Board of Missions by the commissioner to the General Assembly, in 1840, that at least one missionary should be sent that year to labor within the bounds of the presbytery.

At the spring meeting of the presbytery in 1841, the presbytery was divided into four districts for missionary labor. Two ministers were assigned to each district, and the duty laid upon them of performing at least two weeks missionary labor in their several districts before the next stated meeting of presbytery.

This scheme of labor was afterwards modified, but in various ways much missionary labor was done by the members of presbytery.

MEETINGS OF PRESBYTERY.

The meetings of presbytery were made meetings for preaching and holding religious services, and reaching the people through them, as well as for the transaction of ecclesiastical business. Special topics were assigned before hand, and several special discourses were frequently preached during a meeting of presbytery. Presbyteries met generally on Thursday, and continued in session until after the Sabbath. At the second meeting of presbytery at Muncie, in August, 1842, which begun on Thursday night and continued until after Sabbath, it was resolved to hold an intermediate meeting before the regular spring meeting. The time fixed for this meeting was October. It was held with the Lewisville church in Rush county, a church whose name was shortly afterward changed to Ebenezer. The following were the appointments for preaching at this intermediate meeting:

W. Sickles, on "Faith."
D. Monfort, on "Baptism."
P. D. Gurley, on "Prayer."
R. Irwin, on "Repentance."
J. G. Monfort, on "The Judgment."

These intermediate meetings, with preaching upon special topics, were held for several years. They doubtless were designed for accomplishing missionary work.

WHITE WATER PRESBYTERY.

In 1848, the General Assembly, upon overture from the Synod of Indiana, made the line between the States of Indiana and Ohio the line between the Synods of Indiana and Cincinnati. The Synod of Indiana in session at Hanover, October 1848, ordered the formation of the Presbytery of White Water, embracing the counties of Ohio, Dearborn, Ripley, Decatur, Franklin, Rush, Fayette, Union and so much of the counties of Henry and Wayne as lies south of the National road, or in the Presbytery of Indianapolis, except the church at Knightstown.

PRESBYTERY OF MUNCIE.

October, 1848, the Synod of Indiana also ordered the organization of the Presbytery of Muncie. In 1849, the General Assembly made the National Road the dividing line between the Synods of Indiana and northern Indiana. By this action, the First church of Indianapolis and Rev. P. D. Gurley and Rev. W. A. Holliday, were transferred to the Presbytery of Muncie, and the Presbytery of Indianapolis, Old School, was without a church in Indianapolis.

BLOOMINGTON.

By order of Synod in October, 1848, Monroe county, with the church of Bloomington, then in the Presbytery of New Albany, was added to the Presbytery of Indianapolis. Levi Hughes, pastor elect of the church of Bloomington, a licentiate of Presbytery of New Albany, was also received. He was ordained and installed pastor November 3d, 1848.

OWEN AND PUTNAM COUNTIES.

The Synod in 1849, further enlarged the presbytery by adding to it Owen county, and the part of Putnam county south of the National Road with the church of Vandalia, and Rev. Thomas Whallon.

CHAPTER VII.

View of the Field from Reports of Indiana Gazetteer— Number of Old and New School Churches and their increase in Membership—Progress and Prosperity of the country.

LOOKING at the field occupied by the present Presbytery of Indianapolis, we find from the imperfect sketches of the Indiana Gazetteer, published in 1849, the following statements respecting the occupation of this field by other denominations. These statements, combined with the United States census reports of 1850, will give us a more thorough knowledge of the field and its religious condition than we can perhaps otherwise obtain. There is no statement made of the churches and ministers in Bartholomew county. Its population in 1850 was 12,486. In Brown county, "there are six churches, one for each of the denominations of Presbyterians, Methodists, United Brethren, Christian, (or Campbellite) Old Christian, (or New Light,) and Baptists." The population was 4,846. In Hancock county there are "twelve churches, mostly belonging to the Methodists and Baptists." There are "five lawyers, fourteen physicians, thirteen preachers." The population was 9,686. In Hendricks county, "the prevailing religious denominations are Methodists, Baptists, Christians, Friends, Presbyterians and Lutherans." There are thirty-six churches and twenty ministers of the Gospel. The lawyers number six, and physicians twenty. The population is 14,083.

In Johnson county there are "twenty-two churches, mostly belonging to the Baptists, Methodists and Presbyterians." There are "five lawyers, twenty-one physicians, twenty-nine preachers." The population was 12,100. Marion county is described as having "forty lawyers, fifty physicians, forty preachers and thirty-six churches, of which the Methodists are most numerous, then follow Baptists, Christians, Presbyterians, Lutherans, Friends, Episcopalians, Catholics, Seceders, Universalists, etc." The population of Marion county in 1850, was 24,103. Of Morgan county it is said "the religious denominations which have erected churches are as follows: Cumberland Presbyterians one, Lutherans one, Baptists five, Reformers or Christians ten, Friends three, Methodists fourteen." There are "seven lawyers, twenty physicians, thirty preachers." The population was 14,576. Of Monroe county the chronicler facetiously remarks, there are "nine lawyers, ten physicians, and preachers too *tedious* to mention." No mention is made of the churches in the county. There were some eight Baptists, nine Christian and twelve Methodist churches. One Presbyterian, two Cumberland Presbyterian, one Associate, one Associate Reformed, one Old Side Covenanter, one New Side Covenanter. The population was 11,286. In Putnam county there were "twenty-nine Methodist, fifteen Baptist, twelve Christian and five Presbyterian churches." The population was 18,615. As to the number of ministers reported in the Gazetteer, the author in his Introduction says: "It may be said that from the number of preachers of the gospel represented to be found in the various counties, it will be supposed there is much more religious instruction given than is actually the case. The *quality* is perhaps the only thing in dispute. A part of it is not inferior to any other, but a part too, was correctly described by one who, when receiving furs and skins for his salary, was asked 'whether it was not poor pay?' 'Yes,' he said, 'but he gave poor preaching in return.'"

In this field there were, in 1850, twenty-four Presbyterian churches; thirteen New School, eleven Old School. In these churches there were eighteen hundred and fifty-nine members; nine hundred and twenty-five New School, and nine hundred and thirty-four Old School. In 1838, the membership was one thousand and forty-two. In 1850, the increase had become eighty per cent. The population had increased from eighty-four thousand in 1840, to something more than one hundred and twenty thousand in 1850, an increase of something less than fifty per cent for that time.

But the mere increase of population does not mark the real progress and prosperity of this region of country. The construction of railroads and telegraphs opens a new era of activity and enterprise. In 1838, when the great division of the Presbyterian Church occurred, Indianapolis, although the capital of the State, was but a good country town with a population of twenty-five hundred. In October, 1847, the Madison and Indianapolis railroad was completed and the locomotive first entered the city. City, Indianapolis had become by vote in March, 1847, and in the actual establishment of city government in May, 1847. Six months after the railroad reached Indianapolis the telegraph came, and despatches by the wire were first sent as far east as Richmond May 12, 1848. The population of the city at this time was about six thousand. In 1850 it was a little more than eight thousand.

CHAPTER VIII.

Indianapolis Presbytery, O. S.—Changes in Churches—Ministerial Changes—State of Religion—Missionary Work—Presbyterial Authority—First Church of Indianapolis—Second Church of Greencastle—Numbers.

1850—1860.

FOLLOWING on the history for the next twenty-five years, of the churches and presbyteries within the boundaries of the present presbytery, our limits will forbid anything more than a suggestive outline with a statement of results. · Within the Presbytery of Indianapolis, O. S., we find the following

CHANGES IN CHURCHES.

April, 1852, the organization of the church of Boggstown was reported to presbytery, with a membership of thirty-six.

The Third Church of Indianapolis, having been transferred by the General Assembly of 1852, from the Presbytery of Muncie to the Presbytery of Indianapolis, was, in July, 1852, enrolled among the churches of the presbytery. This church had been organized September, 23, 1851, by a committee of Muncie Presbytery. Eighteen members from the First Church of Indianapolis united in its organization.

April, 1854, the organization of the church of Donaldson, with twenty-nine members, was reported; also, the organization of the Union church, with fourteen members, and of the Greenwood church, with nine members.

September, 1854, the organization of a church at Edinburg, with twenty members, was reported.

September, 1855, the organization of a church at Greenfield, with eighteen members, was reported.

MINISTERIAL CHANGES.

April, 1851, the pastoral relation between Levi Hughes and the church at Bloomington was dissolved, and Mr. Hughes dismissed to the Presbytery of Logansport to accept the call of the First Church of Logansport.

April, 1851, H. I. Coe was dismissed to the Presbytery of Muncie.

James Gallatin was dismissed at the same time to the Presbytery of Cedar, Iowa.

April, 1851, J. A. McKee was received from the Presbytery of Madison. In the following June he was installed pastor at Franklin. April, 1860, this pastoral relation was dissolved, on account of the failing health of the pastor's wife and the necessity of a change of climate. In October, 1860, Mr. McKee was dismissed to the Presbytery of St. Paul.

April, 1851, David Stevenson, a licentiate, was received from the Presbytery of Elizabethtown. He was ordained June, 1851. July, 1852, he was installed pastor of the Third Church, of Indianapolis. October, 1860, this pastorial relation was dissolved on account of the failing health of the pastor.

June, 1851, J. C. Caldwell, a licentiate, was received from the Presbytery of Crawfordsville, and ordained and installed at Shelbyville. He was released from his pastoral charge September, 1856, and dismissed to the Presbytery of St. Paul, April, 1857.

June, 1851, H. L. Vannuys was licensed, and April,

1853, dismissed to put himself under the care of the Presbytery of Lake.

June, 1851, R. M. Overstreet was licensed, ordained in September, 1851, and after laboring in the church of Georgetown and elsewhere in the missionary work of the presbytery, was dismissed in October, 1852, to the Presbytery of Palestine.

July, 1852, C. G. McLain, D. D., was received from the Classis of Montgomery, New York. Dr. McLain established in Indianapolis a large and flourishing school for young ladies, under the name of the McLain Seminary. He died in 1860.

July, 1852, Thomas Alexander was received from the Presbytery of Crawfordsville. He was stated supply of the church in Bloomington. September, 1854, he was dismissed to the Presbytery of Brazos, Texas.

July, 1852, Orlando Clark was licensed. September, 1857, he was dismissed to put himself under the care of the Presbytery of Miami.

October, 1852, E. K. Lynn was received from the Presbytery of New Albany. He was installed at Hopewell in the succeeding November. He was released from his pastoral charge in April, 1853, and dismissed September, 1854, to the Presbytery of Palestine.

April, 1853, Alfred Ryors, D. D., was received from the Presbytery of Hocking. Dr. Ryors was president of the State University at Bloomington. He was dismissed to the Presbytery of Madison April, 1854.

September, 1853, J. L. Martin was received from the Presbytery of Louisville. He labored in the churches of Georgetown and Shiloh for a time, and was dismissed to the Presbytery of Vincennes April, 1855.

December, 1853, David Monfort, a licentiate, was received from the Presbytery of White Water, ordained and installed at Knightstown. He was released from this pastoral charge April, 1858, and in September following dismissed to the Presbytery of White Water.

April, 1855, F. H. L. Laird was received from the Presbytery of New Albany. He was stated supply at Bloomington for a year, and dismissed to the Presbytery of Potosi October, 1856.

April, 1855, A. C. Allen was received from the Presbytery of Crawfordsville, and installed at Hopewell. The pastoral relation was dissolved July, 1859.

September, 1856, Wm. Sickles was received from the Presbytery of Madison.

April, 1857, Lowman Hawes was received from the Presbytery of Milwaukee. He was installed at Bloomington in May following. November, 1857, he was released, and dismissed to the Presbytery of Madison, to accept the call of the First Church of Madison.

April, 1857, Blackburn Leffler was received from the Presbytery of Sangamon. He was dismissed to the Presbytery of Vincennes April, 1859.

April, 1858, John Gilchrist was received from the Presbytery of White Water. He was installed over the church of Sugar Creek June, 1858, for one-half his time.

June, 1858, E. C. Sickles was licensed, and dismissed to put himself under the care of the Presbytery of St. Louis.

April, 1859, L. G. Hay was received from the Presbytery of Allahabad, India.

J. J. Smythe was received at the same time from the Presbytery of Orange. After serving the church at Shelbyville until November, 1860, he was then installed its pastor.

April, 1859, T. M. Hopkins, was received from the

Presbytery of Miami. He was called to the pastorate of the church at Bloomington. After several failures of committees appointed by presbytery for the installation services, he was finally installed in October, 1860.

April, 1860, J. F. Smith was received from the Presbytery of White Water. November, 1860, he was installed pastor of the church of Hopewell.

STATE OF RELIGION.

In September, 1851, mention is made in the records of presbytery of a deplorably low state of religion in most of the churches. Because of this low state of religion, a day of fasting and prayer was appointed. At the following spring meeting, this record is made: "In view of the statements made by brethren, in their conversation on the state of religion in our bounds, of the gracious dealings of the Lord among us, it was moved that we spend a short season in thanksgiving to God for what he had done for our churches, beseeching him at the same time for greater blessings." In September, 1855, record is again made of a very low state of religion in the churches of presbytery. April, 1858, mention is made of greatly increased religious interest, and of large accessions to some of the churches.

The Third church of Indianapolis had steadily grown from its original membership of eighteen in 1851, until in 1860, it reported a membership of one hundred and eighty-two.

The largest church in the presbytery, was the Hopewell church, which reported two hundred and sixty-six members.

MISSIONARY WORK.

During this decade, the presbytery for several successive years sought for an intinerant missionary to supply the vacancies. Not succeeding in this, the members of presbytery, with great diligence and zeal, labored among their destitute churches and fields.

PRESBYTERIAL AUTHORITY.

Nor was the presbytery lacking in the exercise of its control over the churches, when in its judgment such control was demanded. In April, 1857, Rev. J. A. McKee applied for a dissolution of the pastoral relation between himself and the church at Franklin. After hearing the parties, presbytery took the following action:

Resolved, 1st, That the request be not granted.

Resolved, 2d, That the church at Franklin be recommended to strengthen their session by the accession of two or more elders.

Resolved, 3d, That the session be directed to discipline any member of said church who shall continue to pursue a course calculated in their judgment to be divisive or destructive to the peace, unity and purity of the church in Franklin.

Resolved, 4th, That a committee of three be appointed with advisory power to aid the session in carrying out this action, and that the chairman of said committee be directed to make known this action to the church on next Sabbath.

And not only did presbytery resolve, but at its fall session, upon report of the committee it had appointed, it proceeded to discipline. The benefits of this maintenance of the order and discipline of the church by the presbytery, are manifest from the concluding paragraph of a page of Judge Banta's history of the church of Franklin. He thus speaks of Mr. McKee's labors: "The year following Rev. Mr. McKee's entry upon his labors here, the membership of the church went down to one hundred and fifteen—twenty-nine members having been dismissed, and seven having died. But in 1852, the gains began to exceed the losses, and with the exception of two years, this has been the case ever since. In that year a refreshing revival came to bless the labors of the new pastor. The good work seems to have commenced in the last of February, and it continued up to the middle of April, during which interval forty persons in all were added on profession of their faith. In the spring of the succeeding year, another shower came, and twenty-five converts were added, which, with the addition of those who joined on certificate, brought the membership up to one hundred and eighty six, the highest number then ever reached. In 1854, the number was carried up to one hundred and ninety-four, but this increase was mostly due to the admissions on certificate. It is evident to one who peruses the records of this date, that a church trouble is again brewing. What the cause was, I am sure I don't know. All I can say is, that in 1854, only five converts were added; in 1855, *not one*, in 1856, three, and in 1857, *not one!* Other work seems to have required the attention of the people during these gloomy years. The younger members of the congregation appear to have been seized about this time with a mania for dancing, while the older brethren had more serious business of their own on hand. A tempest had arisen—a controversy was up—a first class church quarrel was on the carpet, and while the brethren were cutting and threshing this way and that way at each other, no recruits ventured to come from the enemy without. How eloquently do these mute figures plead for *peace* within the church!"

The paragraph of Judge Banta's history immediately succeeding to these statements, is that which shows the benefits of the watchful care of the presbytery and its maintenance of the order and discipline of the church. "In 1858," continues this historian of the Franklin church, "the smoke of this conflict having disappeared, God smiled again upon the labors of Mr. McKee, and in February, March and April of that year, fifty-eight were added on examination."

FIRST CHURCH OF INDIANAPOLIS.

The Rev. John A. McClung, D. D., of Maysville, Kentucky, was installed as pastor of this church December 31, 1851. This relation continued until dissolved, September, 1855, on account of ill health of the pastor. The Rev. Thomas M. Cunningham, of St. Louis, was called as pastor December 12, 1856, and continued until May, 1860. The membership of the church reported in 1860 was two hundred and thirteen.

SECOND CHURCH OF GREENCASTLE.

This church was ministered to by Rev. J. M. McChord for about four years after its organization. He was succeeded by Rev. E. W. Fiske, who began his ministry with the church in 1854. It reported, in 1860, one hundred and ten members.

NUMBERS.

In 1860 the presbytery consisted of eleven ministers and sixteen churches, containing fourteen hundred and forty-one members. Fourteen of these churches, and eleven hundred and ninety members were within the boundaries of the present Presbytery of Indianapolis. In connection with the Old School body, there were also several other churches of Muncie and Crawfordsville Presbyteries, besides the First Church of Indianapolis and Second Church of Greencastle, which are now within the boundaries of the present Presbytery of Indianapolis. These were New Hope, Carpentersville and Clermont. There was also a German church in Indianapolis, which, after appearing for a series of years in the reports of Muncie Presbytery, disappears. The total of the membership of the Old School churches is one thousand seven hundred and forty.

CHAPTER IX.

Indianapolis Presbytery, N. S. — New Churches — Second Church of Indianapolis — Fourth Church of Indianapolis — Greenwood — Ministerial Changes — Missionary Work — Danville, White Lick, Greencastle, Putnamville, Bainbridge, Bloomington, Columbus.

1851—1860.

APRIL, 1851, the organization of the Second Church of Franklin, with a membership of twenty two, was reported to presbytery.

In the spring of 1851, because of the blessing of God upon the labors of C. E. Babb, pastor of the Second Church of Indianapolis, the church edifice became too small for the congregation, and it became a question with the church whether to enlarge their building or to colonize and form another church. The pastor advised the latter. In presbytery, which convened September 4, 1851, Mr. Babb reported that there was great need of another church in Indianapolis, and that efforts were being made to organize another church. In consequence of this report presbytery passed the following resolution:

That we respectfully recommend to the Second Presbyterian Church of Indianapolis, to take into consideration the propriety and importance of forming another church of our order in that city; and, that if they should embark in such an enterprise, they shall have our sympathy and co-operation.

After a full interchange of opinion, September 30, 1851, the session of the Second Church resolved that it was desirable and practicable to form a colony and organize another Presbyterian church. On the 30th of November, 1851, twenty-four persons, dismissed from the Second Church, were organized into the Fourth Presbyterian Church of Indianapolis.

September, 1857, the organization of the church at Zionsville, with six members and one elder, was reported to presbytery.

April, 1860, the Second Presbyterian Church of Madison county, with ten members, was reported to presbytery.

SECOND CHURCH OF INDIANAPOLIS.

On account of failing health, the Rev. C. E. Babb was released from pastoral care of this church January 31, 1853. April, 1854, he was dismissed to the Presbytery of Cincinnati.

The church remained vacant a full year. January 1, 1854, Rev. Thornton A. Mills, to whom a call had been extended by the church the previous October, entered upon the duties of the pastorate. He was received from the Presbytery of Cincinnati, and installed February, 1854. Under the ministry of Dr. Mills the church steadily grew, although there were no seasons of revival. February, 1857, Dr. Mills was released from pastoral charge of the church, to enter upon the duties of Secretary of the General Assembly's Committee on Education, to which he had been elected towards the close of the year 1856. August, 1857, the church gave a call to the Rev. George P. Tindall. Having accepted the call, he was received by the presbytery from the Presbytery of Dayton, October, 1857, but was not installed until June, 1859. The year 1858 was a year of revival throughout the land. The Second Church, from April, 1858, to April, 1859, received to its membership fifty-three on profession of faith and sixteen by letter. The membership reported in 1860 was one hundred and ninety-five.

FOURTH CHURCH OF INDIANAPOLIS.

The Fourth Church in the beginning of 1852, secured for its minister the Rev. George M. Maxwell. He was received from the Presbytery of Franklin, August, 1852. He first served the church as stated supply. He became pastor elect April, 1854, and was installed February, 1856. On account of failing health, he was released from his pastoral charge, December, 1858, and dismissed to the Presbytery of Cincinnati April, 1860.

During the ministry of Mr. Maxwell in the Fourth Church, after nearly six years of struggle, the church dedicated its first house of worship at the corner of Delaware and Market streets. Its membership, at that time, had increased to one hundred and fifteen. In the spring of 1858 a large accession was reported of thirty-three by profession and twenty by letter.

October, 1859, A. L. Brooks was called to the church. He entered upon his labors immediately, and was received by the presbytery from the Presbytery of Chicago, April, 1860. The church reported in April, 1860, only eighty-five members.

GREENWOOD.

The pastor of the Greenwood church, P. S. Cleland, continued steadily on in his labors through this decade in the history of the presbytery, and the second decade of his labors with the Greenwood church. September 17, 1853, the third house of worship erected by the congregation, was dedicated to the worship of God. The year 1853 was marked by a season of special religious interest. There was also a revival in 1856, resulting in larger additions to the church than at any other time during the ministry of Mr. Cleland. Twenty-eight persons were received upon profession of their faith. In 1860, there was reported a membership of one hundred and twenty-six.

MINISTERIAL CHANGES.

To those already mentioned as occurring in this period of the history of the presbytery, the following are to be added:

April, 1851, E. Scofield was received from the Presbytery of Cincinnati. He was at different times supply of the Highland and Second Franklin churches; also of Pendleton, Anderson and Greenfield. These were all missionary churches, with a membership of three, in the smallest reported, Pendleton, and of twenty-three in the largest, Highland. Mr. Scofield was dismissed to the Presbytery of Hamilton, September, 1853. September, 1858, he was again received from the Presbytery of Hamilton, and ministered to the church at Anderson.

April, 1851, Mr. Nyce was dismissed to Felicity Presbytery.

September, 1851, J. Fairchild was received from the Presbytery of Crawfordsville. His labors were first in Hancock county. He afterwards was supply of the Highland and Second Franklin churches. September, 1856, he was dismissed to the Presbytery of Ft. Wayne.

August, 1852, John Stewart was received from the Presbytery of Lexington. April, 1853, he was dismissed to the Presbytery of Madison.

April, 1853, W. A. McCampbell was received from the Presbytery of Green River. He became stated supply of New Providence or Southport. He was permitted to labor in his new field but a few months. He was removed by death, August, 1853.

April, 1853, J. Brownlee was received from the Presbytery of Madison. He was installed pastor of the church at Connersville, June, 1853. April, 1855, he was released from the pastoral care of the church. September, 1859, he was dismissed to the Presbytery of Kansas, having previously labored for some time without the bounds of the presbytery.

September, 1853, B. F. Cole was released from the pastoral care of the churches of Thorntown and Bethel, and dismissed to the Presbytery of Pataskala.

September, 1854, W. R. Stevens was received from the Presbytery of Trumbull. He became supply of Thorntown and Bethel. September, 1856, he was dismissed to the Association of Minnesota.

April, 1855, W. H. Rogers was dismissed to the Presbytery of Salem. His principal field of labor in the presbytery had been Noblesville.

April, 1855, S. E. Wishard was licensed. April, 1857, he was dismissed to put himself under the care of the Presbytery of Schuyler.

September, 1855, A. S. Avery was dismissed to the Presbytery of Alton. He had been for several years without a charge.

September, 1855, W. A. McCorkle was received from the Presbytery of Crawfordsville. April, 1856, he was dismissed to the Presbytery of Fox River.

April, 1856, Philander Anderson was received from the Presbytery of Fort Wayne. He remained in the presbytery without charge.

September, 1856, E. B. Smith was received from the Presbytery of Harmony. He supplied the church of

Connersville, and September, 1857, was dismissed to the Presbytery of Clinton.

September, 1856, George H. White, a licentiate of Fourth Hartford Association, was received. He was ordained an evangelist November, 1856, and went as a missionary to Turkey under appointment from the American Board of Foreign Missions.

October, 1857, Franklin Putnam was received from the Presbytery of Dayton. He became stated supply of Thorntown and Bethel. While engaged in this field, he was removed by death in the summer of 1859, and so ceasing from labor entered into heavenly rest.

September, 1858, J. O. Blythe was received from an Independent church of Philadelphia. September, 1860, he was dismissed to the Third Presbytery of Philadelphia.

September, 1859, D. A. Bassett was received from the Presbytery of Madison. He became stated supply of the church at Connersville.

September, 1860, W. N. Stimson was dismissed to the Presbytery of Greencastle. He had been for several years without charge, but for several years before supply of New Pisgah and Sugar Creek.

September, 1860, Isaac De La Mater was received from the Presbytery of Crawfordsville. He became stated supply of Thorntown and Bethel.

MISSIONARY WORK.

Presbytery labored faithfully to supply the vacancies and destitutions of their field. Strenuous exertions were made to supply vacant churches with the stated ministry of the word at least a portion of the time. The missionaries of the presbytery generally had in charge several small churches. The larger part of the funds for the prosecution of the missionary work within the bounds of the presbytery, was raised within the presbytery. The balance was supplied through the American Home Missionary Society.

The salaries paid the missionaries were but meagre, while their hardships were many. One received two hundred and seventy-five dollars a year; one hundred from the Home Missionary Society, and one hundred and seventy-five from two churches. Another missionary had a salary promised of three hundred and seventy-five dollars; one hundred and seventy-five from the Home Missionary Society, two hundred from two churches. Of this two hundred promised, the churches would fall short fifty dollars. Another brother had five hundred a year, paid to him quarterly by a member of the Second Church. Had this good brother of the Second Church continued to be responsible for a series of years for that necessary support of a missionary, which the field itself could not be made to yield, doubtless the region occupied instead of continuing a moral and spiritual wilderness to so large an extent as it is at the present time, would have been like a garden of the Lord.

But while missionaries were thus laboring on scanty stipends, city ministers received but eight hundred dollars a year. This, however, was paid quarterly, not as it happened, and all paid, and not simply a considerable portion of it.

In 1859 the Synod of Indiana transferred the church of Laurel Hill and the county of Franklin from the Presbytery of Madison to the Presbytery of Indianapolis. The church of Laurel Hill was a feeble church of ten members, and this transfer of the synod only widened the missionary ground of the synod.

DANVILLE.

In Danville, Hendricks county, Presbytery of Greencastle, the Rev. Amos Jones continued his ministry until March, 1853. He was succeeded by Rev. B. F. Cole, who labored in the church for three years. The summer after the departure of Mr. Cole, Rev. S. E. Wishard ministered to the church. Rev. H. L. Dickerson became supply of the church in the fall of 1857. A new church building was dedicated in December, 1858. March 31, 1860, Mr. Dickerson was called to the pastorate of the church. The membership reported in 1860 was one hundred and seven.

WHITE LICK.

The church of White Lick, which was organized from members of the Danville church, first appears on the roll of presbytery in 1854. Its membership increased from twelve in 1854, to thirty-eight in 1860.

GREENCASTLE.

The first church of Greencastle was ministered to by Rev. T. M. Oviatt, from 1851 to 1855. He was succeeded by Rev. Henry Rossiter. In 1860, the membership reported was one hundred and six.

PUTNAMVILLE AND BAINBRIDGE.

Putnamville was ministered to by Rev. Ransom Hawley one-fourth of his time. It enjoyed a season of revival in 1852. Its membership in 1860 was forty.

The Bainbridge church, which was in connection with the Crawfordsville Presbytery, N. S., reported in 1860 a membership of eighty-nine.

BLOOMINGTON.

In June, 1852, a Presbyterian church, New School, was organized, with eleven members, in Bloomington. This church was in connection with the Presbytery of Salem. It was ministered to statedly, by Rev. John M.

Bishop, a portion of his time. After 1854, Professor Elisha Ballantine, of the State University, supplied it for several years upon the alternate Sabbaths, upon which Mr. Bishop was absent. The membership reported in 1860 was seventy-seven.

COLUMBUS.

The church of Columbus, in connection with the Madison Presbytery, N. S., was supplied from 1850 to 1853 by Rev. J. Brownlee. In June, 1853, the Rev. N. S. Dickey became its stated supply. It reported in 1860 a membership of one hundred and twenty-nine.

CHAPTER X.

Numbers—Census Report of the Statistics of the different Denominations in the field occupied by the Presbytery.

In the Presbytery of Indianapolis, N. S., there were, in 1860, twelve ministers, eighteen churches, and eight hundred and three members. Of these eighteen churches, only nine were within the boundaries of the present Presbytery of Indianapolis. Of these nine churches, five were small, aggregating only sixty-seven members. The other four churches contained a membership of four hundred and fifty-seven. The membership of the nine churches was five hundred and four. In the seven other New School churches that were within the bounds of the present Presbytery of Indianapolis, there was a membership of five hundred and eighty six, making a total membership in the New School churches of eleven hundred and ten.

This number, added to the seventeen hundred and forty of the Old School churches, would make the membership of the Presbyterian churches within the boundaries of the present presbytery to have been, in 1860, two thousand eight hundred and fifty.

This is not so rapid an increase of the members of the Presbyterian church upon this field as in the preceding ten years of its history. It is only an increase of little more than fifty per cent., while the increase of the preceding decade was eighty per cent. But the rate of

PRESBYTERY OF INDIANAPOLIS.

increase is greater than that of the population. The population of the counties within the presbytery increased from a little more than a hundred and twenty thousand (121,736) to something over a hundred and fifty-eight thousand (158,853), an increase of little more than thirty-three per cent. In 1850, the proportion of the membership of the Presbyterian church in the field of the presbytery was about one to sixty-five of the population. In 1860, the proportion is one to fifty-five.

CENSUS REPORT.

The United States census report of 1860, more complete and accurate than that of 1870, gives the following religious statistics of the field occupied by the presbytery:

Bartholomew county, with a population of 17,865, has—

3 Presbyterian churches, with property valued at $1,450.
9 Baptist " " " " " 7,750.
6 Christian " " " " " 7,650.
1 Friends' " " " " " 1,200.
4 Lutheran " " " " " 1,900.
1 Moravian " " " " " 3,500.
25 Methodist " " " " " 17,800.

Brown county, with a population of 6,504, has—

1 Presbyterian church, with property valued at $400.
9 Baptist " " " " " 600.
3 Christian " " " " " 420.
6 Methodist " " " " " 2,450.

Hancock county, with a population of 12,802, has—

2 Christian churches, with property valued at $3,700.
2 Baptist " " " " " 800.
6 Lutheran " " " " " 3,750.
14 Methodist " " " " " 8,000.
3 Union " " " " " 1,054.
1 Presbyterian " no property.

Hendricks county, with a population of 16,953, has—

4 Presbyterian churches, with property valued at	$10,000.
11 Baptist " " " " "	4,750.
9 Christian " " " " "	6,400.
4 Friends' " " " " "	14,000.
11 Methodist " " " " "	3,700.

Johnson county, with a population of 14,854, has—

9 Presbyterian churches, with property valued at	$15,450.
16 Baptist " " " " "	10,375.
11 Christian " " " " "	8,300.
18 Methodist " " " " "	10,125.
1 Roman Catholic " " " " "	400.

Marion county, with a population of 39,855, has—

9 Presbyterian churches, with property valued at	$92,960.
10 Baptist " " " " "	31,200.
3 Christian " " " " "	4,600.
1 Congregational " " " " "	8,000.
1 Episcopalian " " " " "	27,000.
5 Friends' " " " " "	6,500.
1 Lutheran " " " " "	800.
32 Methodist " " " " "	100,905.
2 Roman Catholic " " " " "	19,000.

Monroe county, with a population of 12,847, has—

2 Presbyterian churches, with property valued at	$10,500.
9 Baptist " " " " "	3,500.
10 Christian " " " " "	5,000.
13 Methodist " " " " "	14,100.
1 Cumb'rl'nd Pr. " " " " "	800.
2 Reformed Pr. " " " " "	2,000.
2 United Pr. " " " " "	3,200.

Morgan county, with a population of 16,110, has—

26 Methodist churches, with property valued at	$23,800.
4 Baptist " " " " "	11,800.
12 Christian " " " " "	11,800.
2 Episcopal " " " " "	800.
6 Friends' " " " " "	6,100.
1 Cumb'rl'nd Pr. " " " " "	1,000.
1 Rom'n Catholic " " " " "	300.

Putnam county, with a population of 20,681, has—

8 Presbyterian churches, with property valued at $18,700.
18 Baptist " " " " " 11,690.
14 Christian " " " " " 14,700.
27 Methodist " " " " " 42,350.
2 Cumb'rl'nd Pr. " " " " " 3,200.

The term churches, denoting particular organizations or congregations, gives no definite information concerning the strong or weak, the prosperous or declining condition of particular organizations. Yet the term church, denoting an individual congregation, has definite ideas of organization, of life, of power, of influence, connected with it. And in the absence of more complete knowledge, the United States census report of the number of the churches of the different denominations in the field occupied by our presbytery, and especially in connection with the value of the property possessed by these churches, gives us much valuable information and perhaps clearer and more accurate knowledge of the whole field than can otherwise be obtained by us.

CHAPTER XI.

Indianapolis Presbytery, N. S.—Greenfield Church—Kingston and Clarksburg—Edinburg—Sixth Church of Indianapolis— Shelbyville— Ministerial Changes— Progress— Reunion—Adjournment sine die—Hendricks County— Putnam County—Bloomington—Columbus— Numbers.

1861—1870.

RENEWING our history of the Presbytery of Indianapolis, New School, we will find it in the progress of the next ten years growing in numbers, strength and efficiency.

February, 1861, it received the church of Greenfield, which was at the time in connection with the Old School Presbytery of Indianapolis. It also received J. T. Iddings, a licentiate of the Presbytery of Kaskaskias, O. S., and installed him pastor of the Greenfield church. But at the next meeting of presbytery, in April, citations were issued for the trial of Mr. Iddings, for forgery of the certificate of licensure, upon which he had been received into the presbytery. After long and wearisome trials before presbytery, and in synod, he was found guilty and deposed from the ministry. The church of Greenfield was visited by committees of presbytery at various times, but had become alienated from the presbytery, and in the spring of 1866 reunited with the Old School Presbytery.

May, 1863, the Second Church of Franklin was dissolved, and the stated clerk directed to furnish the remaining members with letters to unite with such branches of the church of Christ as they might elect.

April, 1864, the churches of Kingston (formerly Sand Creek) and Clarksburg were received into the presbytery. They had left the presbytery years before, because the General Assembly had not taken such action upon the subject of slavery as they thought should be taken. They had united with the Felicity Presbytery of the Free Presbyterian Church. The civil war and emancipation proclamation of the President of the United States, by which the system of slavery was destroyed, took away the standing place and removed the necessity of the existence of a Free Presbyterian Church, and these churches now returned to the old fold with a largely increased membership.

September, 1864, the reorganization of a church at Edinburg was reported to presbytery. .

The Sixth Church of Indianapolis, called Olivet at the time of its organization, was established by the Second Church. In June, 1867, a committee was appointed by the Second Church to buy lots and build a chapel in the south-western part of the city. A site was selected at the corner of Union and McCarty streets. A building was begun in September. In October it was completed. The 20th of November a church was organized with twenty-one members. It was reported to presbytery April, 1868. In the spring of 1870 it reported one hundred and eleven members.

April, 1861, presbytery received under its care the First German Church of Shelbyville, with one hundred and twenty-five members.

MINISTERIAL CHANGES.

August, 1861, L. P. Webber, a licentiate of Dayton Presbytery, was received and employed as presbyterial missionary. November, 1861, he was ordained. September, 1863, he was dismissed to the Presbytery of San José.

October, 1861, John S. Craig and John B. Logan, members of the Presbytery of Holston, Tennessee, unable to get their letters from their presbytery on account of the war, were received without them.

Anderson was for a series of years the scene of the labors of J. S. Craig; afterwards Noblesville. J. B. Logan, as stated supply and home missionary, occupied various fields.

April, 1862, A. L. Brooks, stated supply of the Fourth Church of Indianapolis, and D. A. Bassett, stated supply of the church of Connersville, were dismissed to the Presbytery of Chicago.

May. 1863, A. A. Jimeson was received from the Presbytery of Dayton. He was pastor elect of the church at Connersville. April, 1865, he was dismissed to the Presbytery of Sciota.

May, 1863, A. T. Rankin was received from the Presbytery of Ripley. He was stated supply of the Kingston and Clarksburg churches.

September, 1863, C. H. Marshall was received from the South Congregational Association of Illinois. He was stated supply of the Fourth Church of Indianapolis.

September, 1863, T. A. Steele was received from Salem Presbytery. He labored as home missionary for one year, and was dismissed September, 1864, to Salem Presbytery.

September, 1863, G. P. Tindall was released from the

pastoral care of the Second Church of Indianapolis, and dismissed to the Presbytery of Washtenaw.

September, 1864, H. A. Edson was received from the Presbytery of Niagara. He was called to the pastorate of the Second Church of Indianapolis November 5, 1863; began his ministry in the Second Church January 17, 1864, and was installed April 26, 1865.

April, 1865, Joseph Swindt was licensed. He was ordained June, 1866, and dismissed to Ripley Presbytery September, 1866.

March, 1866, W. L. S. Clark was received without credentials. He had been laboring for some months under direction of the Committee on Home Missions. September, 1867, he was dismissed to the Presbytery of St. Louis.

September, 1866, Isaac De La Mater was dismissed to the Presbytery of Hamilton. He had labored for several years as stated supply of the church at Thorntown, and in 1863 was commissioned chaplain of the seventy-second regiment of Indiana volunteers.

December, 1866, the pastoral relation of P. S. Cleland and the church at Greenwood was dissolved, after a ministry of twenty-six years, ten as stated supply and sixteen as pastor. The reason for the dissolution of the pastoral relation urged by Mr. Cleland was impaired health, that made it perilous for him to continue his pastoral labors, and impossible for him to discharge the duties of pastor. Mr. Cleland, who had become stated clerk of presbytery in 1859, continued to discharge the duties of stated clerk until April, 1869. In September, 1869, after laboring thirty years within the bounds of the presbytery, his labors at Greenwood antedating the organization of the presbytery, he was dismissed to the Presbytery of Smoky Hill, Kansas.

April, 1867, Alexander Parker was received from the Presbytery of Madison. He was stated supply of the church at Connersville.

April, 1867, George D. Parker was licensed. He was ordained October, 1867, labored at Edinburg, and was dismissed to Vincennes September, 1869.

April, 1867, Thomas G. Bartholomew was licensed, ordained April, 1869, and dismissed to the Presbytery of Lansing April, 1870.

September, 1867, Horace Bushnell, Jr., was received from the Presbytery of Madison, and became stated supply of the Southport church.

April, 1868, J. B. Brandt was received from the Presbytery of Wabash. His first work was in connection with the Sixth church of Indianapolis.

Rufus Nutting, Jr., was received at the same time from the Presbytery of Illinois, and G. H. White dismissed to Windsor Association, Vermont.

April, 1868, Alexander Reid was received from the Presbytery of Madison, and installed pastor of the church at Anderson.

April, 1868, Frederick F. Friedgen was received from the Presbytery of Madison. He was stated supply of the First German Church of Shelbyville.

December, 1868, Luman A. Aldrich was received from the Presbytery of Cincinnati, and installed pastor of the Sixth Church of Indianapolis.

September, 1869, H. L. Dickerson was received from the Presbytery of Greencastle. He became stated supply of the church at Edinburg.

July 2, 1870, J. H. Eschmeier was received from the Indiana Classis of the German Reformed Church, and installed pastor of the First German Church of Shelbyville.

DEATHS.

September 9, 1866, Claiborne Young, one of the oldest members of the presbytery, died at his own residence in Boone county, at the age of sixty-six.

June 19, 1867, Thornton A. Mills, D. D., Secretary of the General Assembly's Committee on Education, fell dead from a stroke of apoplexy as he was stepping from the ferryboat at Hoboken, New Jersey. So, absent from the body, he entered into the presence of the Lord.

PROGRESS.

During this period of ten years, the years 1866, 1867 and 1870 were marked with the greatest increase to the churches. The narrative for 1866 says: "We desire to express our gratitude to God for the increased prosperity of many of our churches since the last report to presbytery. The influence of the numerous revivals during the last winter is apparent in the large and attentive congregations, the earnest prayer meetings, and the growing Sabbath schools, of which not a few are able to speak." The revivals of 1868 prevailed in a larger number of the churches, and resulted in large additions. In 1870, two of the churches of the presbytery were blessed with very large additions. The church of Kingston received one hundred and twenty-two upon profession of faith; the Second Church of Indianapolis one hundred and twenty-six.

During this period, the Second Church of Indianapolis began and completed its second house of worship. Ground was broken for the structure at the corner of Pennsylvania and Vermont streets in the spring of 1864. The corner-stone was laid May 14, 1866; the chapel was first occupied December 22, 1867, and the completed edifice was dedicated January 9, 1870. The entire cost of the property was about one hundred and five thousand dollars.

REUNION.

The first mention made of reunion in the records of presbytery is in April, 1865. Then, Rev. Wm. Phelan is present as a delegate from White Water Presbytery, and presents to the presbytery a series of resolutions from the White Water Presbytery on the subject of the reunion of the two branches of the Presbyterian church. The following resolutions were passed by the presbytery :

First. That the presbytery cordially reciprocate the sentiments and action of the White Water Presbytery on the subject of the union of the now divided Presbyterian church.

Second. That we instruct our commissioners to the next General Assembly to co-operate in any measures which may be proposed in the Assembly which, in their judgment, may have a tendency to bring about a harmonious and honorable blending of the two branches of the Presbyterian church.

Third. That Rev. A. A. Jimeson and Elder P. H. Roots be appointed to convey to the White Water Presbytery, either in person, or otherwise, our sincere Christian salutations, and our willingness to co-operate in bringing about a union so desirable.

Fourth. That Rev. C. H. Marshall and Elder W. N. Jackson be appointed delegates to the Indianapolis Presbytery, O. S., which is to meet in Indianapolis next week, and extend to that body our fraternal greetings and our readiness for an organic union with their branch of the church as soon as in the providence of God the way is open.

The final action of the presbytery on the subject of reunion is in September, 1869.

An overture on the reunion of the two branches of the Presbyterian church, O. S. and N. S., was received from the General Assembly, through its stated clerk, propounding the following question, and directing that a report to the Assembly of the answer given should be made before November 1, 1869:

"Do you approve of the reunion of the two bodies claiming the name and rights of the Presbyterian church in the United States of America, on the following basis, namely:

'The reunion shall be effected on the doctrinal and ecclesiastical basis of our common standards: the Scriptures of the Old and New Testaments shall be acknowledged to be the inspired word of God, and the only infallible rule of faith and practice; the Confession of Faith shall continue to be sincerely received and adopted as containing the system of doctrine taught in the Holy Scriptures; and the Government and Discipline of the Presbyterian church in the United States shall be approved as containing the principles and rules of our polity.'"

The vote being taken on this overture, it was answered in the affirmative by a unanimous rising vote, and presbytery directed that a special record should be made of the names of all voting. The list follows:

MINISTERS.	CHURCHES.	ELDERS.
Philip S. Cleland		
John S. Craig	Noblesville	H. F. Chappell.
Charles H. Marshall	Indianapolis, 4th	Samuel Merrill.
John B. Logan	Edinburg	Henry Ewing.
Rufus Nutting, Jr.		
Philander Anderson		
Alexander Parker		
Henry L. Dickerson	Thorntown	John Higgins.
Archibald S. Reid	Anderson, 1st	Jacob Beachler.
Arthur T. Rankin	Kingston	J. B. Hopkins.
Francis F. Friedgen	Shelbyville, Ger	Henry Burkher.
Hanford A. Edson	Indianapolis, 2d	Edwin J. Peck.
Horace Bushnell, Jr.	Southport	Samuel Moore.
	Greenwood	Garret Sorter.
Luman A. Aldrich	Olivet	C. P. Wilson.
John B. Brandt		

FINAL ADJOURNMENT.

July 3, 1870, at the close of installation services in the First German church, in Shelbyville, "the Presbytery of Indianapolis, N. S., as existing prior to the reunion, adjourned *sine die*, with thankfulness to God for all the good it had been permitted to do, and for that union, which gives hope for greater good in the future."

HENDRICKS COUNTY.

The Danville church enjoyed the ministry of W. L. Dickerson until February, 1868, when the pastoral relation was dissolved by the Presbytery of Greencastle. W. L. Lee succeeded to the pastorate of the church July, 1868. The number reported in the church, 1870, was one hundred and forty-four.

The church at White Lick reported at the same time sixty-three.

PUTNAM COUNTY.

The Rev. Henry Rossiter ministered to the church at Greencastle until December, 1868. W. A. Bosworth became, in 1869, supply, and was supply for one year.

In January, 1864, a new house of worship, begun some years before, was dedicated to the worship of God. The membership in 1869 was one hundred and four. Organic union with the Second church had been completed in the spring of 1870, and a membership of two hundred and fifty is reported in connection with the Presbytery of Crawfordsville, O. S. In the Second church there was, in 1869, one hundred members.

The Bainbridge church reported in 1870, seventy members.

In 1865, the Rev. Ransom Hawley ceased his labors in the Putnamville church as stated supply. When he ceased his labors, he had been ministering to the church one-fourth of his time for twenty-four years. Rev. John Hawks became stated supply of the Putnamville church for one-fourth of his time. The membership reported in 1870, was eighty-nine.

BLOOMINGTON.

The church at Bloomington was supplied by Rev. John M. Bishop one-half of his time until 1865, when he was installed as pastor by the Salem Presbytery. Until this installation, Prof. Ballantine supplied the church one-half the time. In the fall of 1867, Mr. Bishop was released from the pastorate of the church, to accept a call to the church at Rockville. Prof. Ballantine at this time, became stated supply of the church and ministered to it for two years. In the fall of 1869, this church, the Second Presbyterian church of Bloomington, made arrangements for united services with the First church. These services continued until April, 1870, when the organic union of the First and Second churches was consummated. The Second church had at the time of this union, a membership of sixty-eight.

COLUMBUS.

This church was ministered to by Rev. N. S. Dickey, until November, 1870, when he terminated his labors with the church, closing a ministry to it of seventeen years. The membership reported in 1870, was one hundred and seventy.

At the time of the final adjournment of the Indianapolis Presbytery, N. S., there were connected with it, fifteen ministers and nineteen churches, with a membership of nineteen hundred and fifty-nine. Of these churches, eight are within the bounds of the present presbytery, and had a membership of one thousand and thirty-six. The other seven churches that were in connection with New School presbyteries, had a membership of six hundred and seventy three. The total membership of all the churches, was seventeen hundred and seventeen.

CHAPTER XII.

Indianapolis Presbytery, O. S.—Changes in the Churches —Ministerial Changes—Deaths—State of the Country— Revivals—Reunion—First Church at Indianapolis—Seventh Church of Indianapolis—Brownsburg and Clermont —Greencastle, Carpentersville, Bloomington—Numbers.

1861—1870.

In this last decade of the history of this presbytery, we note first the changes in the churches.

In April, 1861, the Edinburg church was dissolved, and by request of its members they were united with the church at Franklin.

April, 1865, the name of New Providence church was changed to Acton.

April, 1865, the church of Greenwood was dissolved.

April, 1866, the Greenfield church, reporting a membership of one hundred and thirty-eight, was received.

October, 1867, the organization of the Fifth church of Indianapolis with eighteen members, was reported to presbytery.

October, 1867, the church of Bloomington, with its pastor, T. M. Hopkins, was transferred to the Presbytery of New Albany.

MINISTERIAL CHANGES.

April, 1861, A. B. Morey, a licentiate of the Presbytery of Albany was received. The succeeding month of May he was ordained and installed at Franklin.

April, 1861, J. B. Vawter was licensed. March, 1863, he was dismissed to put himself under the care of the Presbytery of Dubuque.

September, 1861, Charles Axtel was received from the Presbytery of Rock River. He was installed at Knightstown in the following October. April, 1864, he was released from his pastoral charge. In September, 1865, he was dismissed to the Presbytery of Dubuque.

September, 1861, P. R. Vanatta was received from the Presbytery of Hillsboro. His labors were in the Bible cause.

September, 1861, G. C. Heckman was received from the Presbytery of Milwaukee. October, 1871, he was installed pastor of the Third church of Indianapolis. This pastoral relation was dissolved in October, 1867, and Dr. Heckman dismissed to the Presbytery of Albany to accept a call from the State Street Church, Albany.

June, 1862, B. F. Wood was released from the pastoral care of the Bethany church.

June, 1862, F. Senour was received from the Presbytery of Louisville. March, 1863, he was dismissed to the Presbytery of Chicago.

June, 1862, J. H. Vannuys, a licentiate of the Presbytery of Donegal, was received. April, 1863, he was dismissed to put himself under the care of the Presbytery of Rock River.

September, 1862, Levi Hughes was received from the Presbytery of St. Paul. This brother losing his hearing, and becoming entirely deaf by exposure while preaching in Minnesota, became, notwithstanding this great affliction of being totally deaf, an earnest and successful evangelist. He labored for some time as evangelist and missionary in the presbytery, and then became agent for Hanover College. He was dismissed to the Presbytery of New Albany in October, 1867.

April, 1863, W. W. Sickles was received from the Presbytery of New Albany.

April, 1864, J. Q. McKeehan was received from the Presbytery of Madison. May, 1869, he was dismissed to the same presbytery.

C. H. Raymond was received at the same time from the Presbytery of White Water. April, 1866, he was dismissed to the Presbytery of Oxford.

April, 1865, S. E. Barr was received from the Presbytery of New Albany. May following he was installed at Hopewell.

April, 1865, N. S. Palmer was received from the Presbytery of Crawfordsville. His labors were principally in connection with the American Tract Society.

April, 1866, James Gilchrist was received from the Presbytery of White Water. He was stated supply of the Bethany church. April, 1870, he was dismissed to the Presbytery of Crawfordsville.

April, 1866, R. B. Abbott was received from the Presbytery of White Water. He was stated supply of the church at Knightstown. In April, 1867, he was dismissed to the Presbytery of St. Paul.

April, 1866, J. J. Smythe was released from the pastoral care of the church at Shelbyville. April, 1867, he was dismissed to the Presbytery of Erie.

September, 1866, R. M. Overstreet was received from the Presbytery of Central Texas.

April, 1867, C. P. Jennings was received from the Presbytery of Logansport. He labored in connection with the church at Shelbyville. Dissatisfied with the reunion of the Presbyterian church, he united with the

Protestant Episcopal church, and his name was dropped from the roll of the presbytery April, 1870.

April, 1867, Isaac W. Monfort was received from the Presbytery of White Water. His labors were in connection with the church at Greenfield.

September, 1867, W. B. Chamberlain, a licentiate of the Presbytery of Madison, was received. He became stated supply of the Fifth Church of Indianapolis, and was ordained October, 1867.

April, 1868, L. B. W. Shryock was received from the Presbytery of New Castle. He was installed at Knightstown in the fall of 1868.

September, 1868, Robert Sloss, a licentiate of the Third Presbytery of New York, was received. Receiving and accepting a call from the Third Church of Indianapolis, he was ordained and installed.

April, 1869, J. C. King was dismissed to the Presbytery of Iowa.

April, 1870, J. R. Walker was received from the Indiana Presbytery of the United Presbyterian church.

DEATHS.

The death of John Gilchrist, pastor of Sugar Creek church, is recorded in the minutes of the sessions of presbytery in April, 1863.

In the minutes of the sessions of presbytery, in September, 1864, the death of William Sickles, at the age of three score and ten, is recorded. Also the death of John F. Smith, in the prime of his life, and pastor of the church at Hopewell at the time of his decease.

STATE OF THE COUNTRY.

September, 1861, the presbytery passed the following resolution:

Resolved, That this presbytery hereby expresses its cordial approval of the resolutions adopted at the late meeting of the Assembly, in regard to the state of the country, and express the hope that the churches under its watch and care will continue instant in prayer, that the constituted authorities of the nation may be sustained in their efforts to suppress this rebellion, and bring the conflict which has been precipitated upon us, to a speedy and successful issue.

The following resolutions were also passed:

Resolved, That we are sensible of the evil effects of the present state of our national affairs upon the kingdom of Christ, and we do earnestly urge upon the churches under our care the necessity of frequent and persevering prayer for the presence of the Holy Spirit to withstand those worldly influences which threaten to secularize the church and render ineffectual the preaching of the word.

Resolved, That we recognize higher relations and duties than those imposed by civil governments, and would therefore earnestly appeal to our brethren in the Southern States to unite with us in supplications to our common King and Saviour, that he may bless our country with a speedy, righteous and permanent peace.

Resolved, That we recommend to all our ministers and churches the propriety of observing the day of prayer appointed by the President of the United States.

April, 1863, the following resolutions were passed:

Resolved, 1st, That presbytery enjoins upon all the churches under its care the full and faithful observance of the day of fasting and prayer, as recommended in the recent proclamation of the President of the United States.

2d. This presbytery, as an ecclesiastical court, called to witness for Christ before the world, cannot refrain a public expression of its gratification that the resolution of the Senate of the United States, asking the appointment of a day of fasting, makes such distinct mention of our Lord Jesus Christ as the heaven-appointed way of access to God the Father. This recognition of our Divine Mediator by our national authorities is as gratifying as it is rare. Our hope for our country grows strong as we see our rulers giving heed to the divine injunction: Be wise, now, therefore, oh, ye kings; be instructed, oh, ye judges of the earth; serve the Lord with fear and rejoice with trembling. Kiss the Son, lest He be angry and ye perish from the way when His wrath is kindled but a little.

REVIVALS.

In the year 1862 a quiet, but efficient work of grace was wrought in many of the churches. Christians were revived. This was the especial feature of the work, a deepening of the piety and a quickening of the activity of Christians. Sinners also were converted. In the church of Hopewell forty were added to the church on the profession of their faith.

In the year 1866 "blessings of more than ordinary magnitude and preciousness" were bestowed upon the majority of the churches. One church received into its membership, upon examination, forty-eight, another thirty-eight, another thirty, another twenty-seven, other churches less numbers.

Of the beginning of 1869 it is said: "During the latter part of April the city of Indianapolis was visited by a remarkable outpouring of God's spirit. During the refreshing which followed in the month of May, June and July, the churches in that city under the control of this presbytery received a special blessing, both in the ingathering of new members and in a general quickening of spiritual life among the members."

In the spring of 1870 it was reported that in nearly all the churches there had been a deep religious interest, and in many of them most remarkable works of grace. In the churches of Franklin and Hopewell, immediately following the week of prayer, God's spirit had been poured out above what they could ask or think.

In the Franklin church one hundred had been received on examination; in the Hopewell church, seventy-seven; in the Fifth Indianapolis, thirty-five; in the Third, one hundred and thirty-two.

REUNION.

April, 1865, Rev. C. H. Marshall and Elder W. N.

Jackson, of the Indianapolis Presbytery, N. S., appeared in the Old School Presbytery, and presented the action their body had taken on the subject of reunion. The following action was taken:

Resolved, 1st, That this presbytery hail with unusual pleasure the presence in our sessions of the brethren, Rev. C. H. Marshall and Ruling Elder W. N. Jackson, corresponding delegates to this body from the Presbytery of Indianapolis, N. S.

2d, That we heartily reciprocate the action of that presbytery looking to a harmonious and honorable blending of the two branches of the Presbyterian church in the United States.

3d, That the Rev. George C. Heckman and Ruling Elder James Blake be appointed principals, and Rev. A. B. Morey and Professor Daniel Kirkwood their alternates, as delegates to convey our Christian salutations and brotherly love to the Presbytery of Indianapolis, N. S., at its next stated meeting at Edinburg, on the 15th of September next, with the expression of our earnest, prayerful desire for an organic union between our respective bodies, when such shall be the will of our Lord Jesus Christ.

As the subject of reunion came up time after time in its progress toward consummation, there were various discussions, and various resolutions were passed. The record of the final and decisive vote in September, 1869, in response to the action of the General Assembly, is: Resolved, That we answer the overture of the General Assembly on the subject of reunion of the two bodies claiming the name and rights of the Presbyterian church in the United States, in the affirmative. Ayes, 15; nay, 1.

FIRST CHURCH OF INDIANAPOLIS.

The Rev. J. Howard Nixon, of the Presbytery of Troy, was called to the pastorate of this church, December 17, 1860. This pastoral relation was dissolved April 14, 1869. The Rev. R. D. Harper, D. D., was called April 22, 1869. The membership of the church in 1870, was three hundred and fifteen.

In the fall of 1864, the foundation of the third church edifice erected by this church was laid at the corner of Pennsylvania and New York streets. The following year the chapel, containing a lecture room and Sabbath School rooms, was erected. The corner stone of the main portion of the building was laid July 23, 1866. The edifice was completed and opened for the worship of God, December 29, 1868. The cost of this building was between one hundred and four and five thousand dollars.

SEVENTH CHURCH OF INDIANAPOLIS.

One Sabbath day, early in the year 1865, Wm. R. Craig, a resident of the south-eastern part of Indianapolis, was much disturbed by a rude and lawless troop of boys. Their repeated and flagrant violations of the Sabbath, and unruly conduct generally, had often outraged the feelings of the staid old Scotchman, but never to such a degree as on this occasion. He now for the first time began seriously to debate with himself the question of a remedy. He finally decided that a Sabbath School, by reaching the consciences of the offenders would, in the course of time, effect a thorough and lasting cure. Being an elder of the First Church, he applied to his brethren for help. They willingly co-operated with him. A Sabbath School was established. Its first session was in the room of a carpenter shop, belonging to Peter Routier, on Cedar street. The number of scholars at the first session was seven. The school rapidly increased. Through the exertions of James M. Ray of the First Church, a site was secured in Fletcher's addition, donated by Calvin Fletcher, Sr., A. Stone, W. S. Witt, Elisha Taylor and James M. Hough. The Board of Church Extension pledged five hundred dollars to the erection of a building, and the First Church took upon itself the responsibilty of carrying the enterprise through. A building was erected at a cost of over three thousand dollars, and December 24, 1865, dedicated to the service of God. The First Church appropriated five hundred dollars to the support of a missionary in the field. W. W. Sickles first undertook the work. Becoming discouraged, he resigned in the spring of 1866. Thomas Galt, a licentiate of Chicago Presbytery and member of the Theological Seminary in Chicago, labored in the field during the summer of 1866. September, 1866, C. M. Howard, from the Presbytery of St. Paul, was invited to occupy the field. November 27, 1867, a church was organized with twenty-three members. Six of these, including an elder, W. R. Craig, were from the First Church. Mr. Craig was the first elder of the Seventh Church. Mr. Howard served the church as stated supply until October, 1869, when, on account of failing health, he withdrew from the field. He was succeeded by Rev. J. B. Brandt, who served one year, when being elected Superintendent of the Young Men's Christian Association of the city, he resigned. He was succeeded by Rev. L. G. Hay. From April, 1868, to April, 1869, sixty-three were added on profession of their faith, and a membership of one hundred and twenty-two reported in the spring of 1869. The membership reported in 1870, was one hundred and forty and four.

BROWNSBURG AND CLERMONT.

The church of Brownsburg was organized in 1867, with seventeen members. It was ministered to by Rev. George Long. It erected a substantial brick edifice, and reported in 1870, a membership of thirty. The neighboring church of Clermont, reported in 1870, a membership of fourteen.

GREENCASTLE.

The Second Church of Greencastle continued under the ministry of Dr. Fisk until the reunion. He then became stated supply of the united church, which reported in 1870, as has been already stated, a membership of two hundred and fifty. The membership of the Second Church reported in 1869, was one hundred. During the winter of 1869 and 1870, eighty persons were received upon profession of faith into the united church.

CARPENTERSVILLE.

The church of Carpentersville reported, in 1870, a membership of seventy-one.

BLOOMINGTON.

In 1863 a new church edifice was dedicated to the worship of God. This church edifice was built under the ministry of T. M. Hopkins, whose energy and zeal in the work were untiring. During the ministry of Mr. Hopkins one hundred and seventeen members were added to the church, sixty-one upon examination, fifty-six by letter. In January, 1869, Mr. Hopkins, accepting a call to the First Church of Piqua, Ohio, was released from the pastorate. In March, 1869, A. Y. Moore, of the Presbytery of Lake, was called to the pastorate. As pastor elect of the First Church and stated supply of the Second, he ministered to the united congregation from October, 1869, to April, 1870. During this time the Spirit of God was poured out upon the people, and thirty-two persons were received into the two churches upon profession of their faith, twenty-five to the First Church, seven to the Second. In April the two churches became united as the Walnut Street Presbyterian Church of Bloomington. A. Y. Moore was called to the pastorate, and installed by the Presbytery of New Albany. The Second Church, during its history, had received into its communion, up to the fall of 1869, one hundred and four persons by examination and seventy-four by letter. At the time of the union of the two churches it had a membership of sixty-eight. Up to October, 1869, there had been received into the communion of the First Church, from the time of its organization, four hundred and eighty-nine persons. Of these, two hundred and sixty were received upon profession of their faith, two hundred and twenty-nine by letter. The membership of the First Church at the time of the union was one hundred and sixty-eight. In the spring of 1870 the Walnut Street Church had a membership of two hundred and thirty-six.

NUMBERS.

In the Presbytery of Indianapolis, O. S., there were, in 1870, eleven ministers and fifteen churches, with a membership of two thousand one hundred and sixty-seven. Of these churches twelve were within the bounds of the present presbytery. They had a membership of eighteen hundred and thirty-one. The other Old School churches in the bounds of the present presbytery aggregated a membership of nine hundred and twenty-six, making a total membership in the Old School churches of two thousand seven hundred and fifty-seven. The membership of the New School churches, within the bounds of the present presbytery, seventeen hundred and seventeen, added to the membership of the Old School churches, gave a membership of four thousand four hundred and seventy-four to the churches within the boundaries of the present presbytery at the time of its organization, July 5, 1870.

The population of the counties within the presbytery was, in 1870, 188,729. It was, in 1860, 158,534. The increase was between twenty-five and thirty-five per cent. The membership of the churches in 1860 was 2,850; in 1870, 4,474. The increase is between forty and fifty per cent. And the proportion of membership to population in 1870 is a fraction less than one to forty-five. In 1860 it was one to fifty-five; in 1850, one to sixty-five. Our church is thus seen to have been growing, not only with the growth of the population of the country, but also at a steady rate of progress more rapidly than that of the population of the country.

CHAPTER XIII.

Indianapolis Presbytery—Its Boundaries, Members and Churches—Changes in Churches—Ministerial Changes—Missionary Work—Women's Presbyterial Society—Revivals—Progress.

1870—1876.

PRESBYTERY OF INDIANAPOLIS.

AFTER the reunion of the Old and New School branches of the Presbyterian church, the Presbytery of Indianapolis, as established by the Synod of Indiana, South, met in the Third Presbyterian church of Indianapolis, at 9 P. M., July 5, 1870, and was called to order and constituted with prayer by Rev. Ransom Hawley, according to the following order of the Synod:

"That the churches located in the counties of Putnam, Hendricks, Marion, Hancock, Johnson, Morgan, Monroe, Brown, Bartholomew, containing about *thirty-two* ministers, be constituted in the Indianapolis Presbytery.

"That the Presbytery of Indianapolis, as this day erected and defined by this Synod, is declared to be, and is the legal successor to the Presbyteries of Indianapolis, O. S., and Indianapolis, N. S., formerly occupying in greater part the same territory; and is entitled to succeed to, and does succeed to all the legal and ecclesiastical rights, privileges, franchises, records, books, papers and property of each of said other presbyteries. And that Rev. R. Hawley be, and he hereby is, appointed convener, to convene, open and constitute said Presbytery of Indianapolis, in this house, this evening at 9 o'clock."

Rev. R. Hawley was elected Moderator, and A. B. Morey Clerk.

The following was the roll of presbytery:

Ministers Present.—B. F. Woods, A. C. Allen, L. G. Hay, A. B. Morey, C. H. Marshall, H. A. Edson, S. E. Barr, N. S. Palmer, H. Bushnell, Jr., W. B. Chamberlain, J. B. Brandt, R. Nutting, L. A. Aldrich, R. Sloss, N. S. Dickey, A. Y. Moore, R. Hawley, A. R. Naylor, R. D. Harper, D. D., E. W. Fisk, D. D.

Ministers Absent.—J. B. Logan, W. W. Sickles, J. W. Monfort, George Long, W. J. Lee, E. Ballantine, J. Greene, E. Wright, C. K. Thompson, John Scott, M. A. Remley.

Churches Represented.—First Indianapolis, W. Sheets; Columbus, C. H. Paddox; Walnut street, Bloomington, James Small; Southport, S. Moore; Greencastle, J. Allen; Second Indianapolis, C. F. Smith; Brownsburg, E. D. Selent; Carpentersville, G. H. McKee; Bainbridge, J. Brown; Third Indianapolis, J. Blake; Fourth Indianapolis, R. M. Stewart; Fifth Indianapolis, E. A. Cobb; Olivet, C. Wilson; Seventh Indianapolis, H. C. Husted.

Churches not Represented.—Franklin, Greenwood, Hopewell, Shiloh, Acton, Highland, Bethany, Danville, Georgetown, New Pisgah, New Prospect, Boggstown, Union, Greenfield, Edinburg, Donaldson, Oak Grove, St. Louis Crossing, New Hope, Clermont, White Lick, Putnamville.

CHANGES IN CHURCHES.

September, 1870, the churches of New Pisgah and New Prospect were consolidated under the name of New Pisgah.

September, 1870, presbytery, by request, provided supplies for Stilesville, in Hendricks county, where a Sabbath school had been organized, but where there was no church of Presbyterian order. At the meeting of presbytery, April, 1871, the organization of a church near Stilesville was reported. It was enrolled as the Hendricks County Church. The name has since been changed to Hebron. A church edifice has been built, and a membership of forty-five was reported April, 1876.

September, 1871, presbytery appointed a committee to organize a church at Indianola. It has received the name of Eighth Presbyterian Church of Indianapolis. The field of this church was first occupied by the Methodists. It was an exceedingly hard field. Having been abandoned by the Methodists, three young members of the Third Presbyterian Church, H. H. Fulton, E. L. Williams and John G. Blake, established a mission Sabbath school in the building that had been occupied by the Methodists. Out of their labors and this mission school grew the Eighth Church. The first report to presbytery, April, 1872, was a membership of twenty-four, eighteen received upon profession of faith and six by letter. April, 1876, the membership was one hundred and twenty-eight.

At a special meeting of presbytery, February, 1872, a committee was appointed to organize the Ninth Presbyterian Church of Indianapolis. April, 1872, the organization of this church was reported, with a membership of twenty. Fourteen had been received by letter, and six upon profession of their faith. The field of this church was first occupied with a Sabbath school organization. It was known as the "Saw Mill Mission." The first school was not prosperous, and becoming extinct, another was established in July, 1870. The leading spirits in the new organization were Gen. Ben. Harrison, Dr. C. C. Burgess, Ebenezer Sharpe, Capt. E. P. Howe,

I. C. Hays and others, all members of the First Presbyterian Church. Rev. L. G. Hay took charge of the mission, and after the organization of the church was its stated supply for several years. The membership reported April, 1876, was one hundred and thirty.

April, 1872, the church of St. Louis Crossing was disbanded.

September, 1872, the Highland church was disbanded.

The Memorial Church was organized March 12, 1873, with thirty-one members, thirty received upon certificate, one upon examination. The origin of Memorial Church is to be traced to the action of the session of the Second Presbyterian Church, in the winter of 1869–'70. It was the desire to signalize the memorial year of Presbyterian reunion by another mission. Lots were purchased and a chapel erected in the north-east quarter of the city, and a Sabbath school established. The enterprise was not at first successful, and it was proposed at one time to sell the property and abandon the mission. But better counsels prevailed. The Young Men's Association of the Second Church was entrusted with the work, and it was prosecuted with vigor, resulting in the organization of the church. April, 1873, Rev. H. A. Edson, released from the pastoral charge of the Second Church, entered upon the labors of the field of the Memorial Church. A site was at once purchased for a permanent church edifice, and contracts let for the building. The corner-stone was laid for the new structure April 7, 1874. The chapel and Sabbath school rooms of the new building were occupied for worship for the first time Sabbath, March 7, 1875. The church has been self-sustaining from the first. It reported April, 1876, a membership of two hundred and eighty-eight.

April 18, 1875, the Eleventh Presbyterian church of

Indianapolis was organized. It reported, April, 1876, a membership of forty, twenty-three had been received by letter, seventeen upon profession of their faith. Rev. B. F. Woods has been stated supply of the church.

June 14, 1876, the Twelfth Presbyterian church of Indianapolis was organized.

MINISTERIAL CHANGES.

The Emperor of Brazil, Dom Pedro, when he saw in Machinery Hall of the Centennial Exposition, the record of the number of the revolutions of the great Corliss engine, more than a million, that had been made from the beginning of its working wittily remarked, "that beats the South American Republics for revolutions." The frequency of changes among the ministers of Indianapolis Presbytery, is a fitting subject for *imperial* wit. An acknowledged evil both to churches and ministers, it manifestly demands a remedy. We note these changes from 1870 to 1876.

September, 1870, I. W. Monfort was dismissed to the Presbytery of St. Paul.

September, 1870, W. J. Lee was released from the pastoral care of the church at Danville. April, 1873, he was dismissed to the Presbytery of Osage, Missouri.

September, 1870, L. A. Aldrich was released from the pastorate of the Sixth church of Indianapolis. September, 1871, he was dismissed to the Presbytery of Cincinnati.

September, 1870, J. G. Williamson was received from the Presbytery of New Albany. He was supply of the Bethany church until failing health disabled him from preaching.

In the fall of 1870, E. W. Fisk, D. D., was installed pastor of the church at Greencastle. This pastoral relation was dissolved April, 1872, that Dr. Fisk might devote his labors to the Female College of Indiana.

October, 1870, W. B. Chamberlain was installed pastor of the Fifth Church at Indianapolis. October, 1872, he was released from this pastoral charge, and dismissed April, 1873, to the Presbytery of Mankato, Minnesota. September, 1875, he was again received from the Presbytery of Mankato, leave given him to labor without the bounds of presbytery, and September, 1876, he was dismissed to the Presbytery of Council Bluffs.

April, 1871, R. D. Harper, D. D., was released from the pastoral care of the First Church of Indianapolis, and dismissed to the Third Presbytery of Philadelphia.

April, 1871, Joseph E. Scott was received from the Presbytery of West Jersey. He was stated supply of the Sixth Church of Indianapolis for one year, and then entered upon the field of Foreign Missions in eastern Turkey.

April, 1871, Alexander Parker was received from the Presbytery of White Water. October, 1871, he was installed pastor of the church at Columbus.

April, 1871, H. L. Dickerson was received from the Presbytery of Crawfordsville. After laboring as stated supply for two years with the Edinburg church, he was dismissed April, 1873, to the Presbytery of Crawfordsville.

April, 1871, N. S. Dickey was dismissed to the Presbytery of Mattoon.

April, 1871, Ambrose Dunn was received from the Presbytery of New Albany. His field of labor since, has been the Greenwood church.

April, 1871, R. B. Herron was received from the Presbytery of Cincinnati. He labored for a season as pastor elect of the Danville church, is now stated supply of Brownsburg and Shiloh.

April, 1871, the pastoral relation between A. B. Morey and the Franklin church was dissolved, and he was dismissed to the Presbytery of Cincinnati, to be installed pastor of the Fifth Church of Cincinnati, a call from which church had at a previous meeting of presbytery been placed in his hands.

June, 1871, C. H. Raymond was received from the Presbytery of Dayton. In the following July, he was installed pastor of the Seventh Church of Indianapolis.

September 1871, J. P. E. Kumler was received from the Presbytery of Vincennes, and in October following, installed pastor of the First Church at Indianapolis. July, 1875, application was made to presbytery by Mr. Kumler, for release from this pastoral charge that he might accept a call to the Third Church of Cincinnati. The First Church of Indianapolis resisted the application of their pastor to the presbytery, and it was not granted. In September the application was renewed by the pastor, and was granted, and he was dismissed to the Presbytery of Cincinnati.

April, 1871, James Williamson was licensed to preach the gospel. October following he was ordained and installed pastor of the churches of Acton and Boggstown. October, 1875, he was released from the pastoral care of the Boggstown church.

April, 1872, S. E. Wishard was received from the Presbytery of Sangamon, and installed pastor of the Franklin church.

April, 1872, J. B. Logan was dismissed to the Presbytery of Crawfordsville. September, 1873, he was again received.

April, 1872, S. S. Bergen was licensed to preach the

gospel. November, 1872, he was ordained an evangelist. April, 1872, he was dismissed to the Presbytery of Austin, Texas.

May, 1872, J. B. Brandt was installed pastor of the Sixth Church of Indianapolis.

May, 1872, John Dixon was licensed to preach the gospel. May, 1873, he was dismissed to put himself under the care of the Presbytery of Boston.

June, 1872, Robert Sloss, accepting a call to the Fourteenth Street Church of New York city, placed by presbytery in his hands, was released from the pastoral care of the Third Church of Indianapolis, and dismissed to the Presbytery of New York.

April, 1873, Augustus L. Williams, a licentiate, was received from the Presbytery of Lansing. He was stated supply of the church at Greencastle for eighteen months. September, 1875, he was dismissed to the Central Presbytery of Philadelphia.

April, 1873, J. A. Williams was received from the Presbytery of Austin. He became supply of the church at Edinburg. September, 1875, he was dismissed to the Presbytery of White Water.

April, 1873, J. R. Mitchell was received from the Presbytery of White Water, and installed pastor of the Fifth Church of Indianapolis.

April, 1873, the pastoral relation of H. A. Edson and the Second Church of Indianapolis was dissolved, and he entered upon his work in the Memorial Church.

September, 1873, E. B. Mason was received from the Puritan Association of Ohio, and installed pastor of the Fourth Church of Indianapolis.

October, 1873, J. L. Withrow, D. D., called by the Second Church of Indianapolis, was received from the Central Presbytery of Philadelphia, and installed. This pastoral relation was dissolved June, 1876, that Dr. Withrow might accept a call to the Park Street Church, Boston.

December, 1873, G. W. F. Birch was received from the Presbytery of Ebenezer, Kentucky, and installed pastor of the Third Church of Indianapolis. This pastoral relation was dissolved June, 1876.

April, 1874, George Long was dismissed to the Presbytery of Logansport.

May, 1874, Lucius I. Root was received from the Presbytery of Mattoon, and installed pastor of the church at Greencastle. This pastoral relation was dissolved, January, 1876, and a letter of dismissal given to Mr. Root to the Presbytery of Alton.

May, 1874, Charles T. White, D. D., was received from the Presbytery of Chemung. He became stated supply of the church at Greenfield, and was dismissed June, 1876, to the Presbytery of White Water.

May, 1874, William Armstrong was received from the Presbytery of Portsmouth.

May, 1874, John R. Sutherland, a licentiate, was received from the Presbytery of Chicago, ordained and installed pastor of the Eighth Church. He was released from this pastoral charge November, 1875, and dismissed to the Presbytery of Grand Rapids.

June, 1874, S. E. Barr was released from the pastoral care of the Hopewell Church, and dismissed to the Presbytery of Fort Wayne.

September, 1874, N. F. Tuck was received from the Presbytery of Louisville.

January, 1875, E. L. Williams was licensed. June, 1876, he was ordained and installed pastor of the Eighth and Twelfth Churches of Indianapolis.

April, 1875, L. F. Walker was received from the Presbytery of Mattoon, and in May following installed pastor of the Ninth Church of Indianapolis.

April, 1875, Edwin Black was received from the Presbytery of Mattoon, and installed pastor of the Hopewell church.

April, 1875, M. M. Lawson was licensed to preach the gospel. September, 1875, he was dismissed to put himself under the care of the Presbytery of Marion.

April, 1875, Henry L. Nave was licensed. June, 1876, he was ordained and installed pastor of the church at Edinburg.

December, 1875, R. J. L. Matthews was received from the Presbytery of Cairo.

April, 1876, E. H. Post was received from the Presbytery of San José. He became supply of the church at Danville.

April, 1876, John H. Harris was received from the Presbytery of Cincinnati. He became supply of the Bethany church.

DEATHS.

Since 1870 four of the members of presbytery have entered, through the gates of death, into the presence and joy of their Lord.

Charles H. Marshall died at Indianapolis, January 27, 1872, at the age of forty-eight.

Charles K. Thompson died at Carlisle, February 8, 1872, at the age of sixty-one.

Edward Wright died at Bloomington, November 10, 1872, at the age of sixty-eight.

N. S. Palmer died at Franklin, November 24, 1873, at the age of fifty-two.

MISSIONARY WORK.

Rev. J. B. Logan was employed in 1870–'71 as presbyterial missionary. By instruction from the presbytery, one result to be aimed at by the missionary was the grouping of feeble churches and combining them in the support of a minister, so that they would require no aid from the Board of Missions. This object having been attained, and the churches supplied with ministers, no new fields outside of Indianapolis opening for occupation, the services of the presbyterial missionary were discontinued at the close of September, 1871.

September, 1876, but two churches were reported as receiving aid from the Board of Missions, the Eleventh Church of Indianapolis and the church of Georgetown.

The amount annually contributed to the cause of home missions, since 1870, has been, on an average, a little more than $3,250. A large portion of this has been expended on mission churches within the city of Indianapolis.

The work of Foreign Missions has not received so large an amount from the churches. The annual contribution from the churches of the presbytery to the cause of Foreign Missions, has been about $2,000.

WOMAN'S MISSION WORK.

September, 1872, a resolution of presbytery earnestly commended the Women's Board of Missions to the sessions and women of the churches of presbytery. In a number of the churches, missionary organizations of the ladies of the churches were formed. September, 1874, the following resolution was passed by presbytery:

Resolved, That we request a committee of three ladies, members of our church, to communicate with all the churches of the presbytery, requesting them to effect the organization of a Woman's Missionary Society, and to secure the appointment of one or more delegates from each church to be present at the next meeting of presbytery.

Mrs. J. P. E. Kumler, of the First Church of Indianapolis, Mrs. J. Clark, of the Franklin church, and Mrs. C. H. Raymond, of the Seventh Church of Indianapolis, were appointed this committee.

At the next stated meeting of the presbytery at Indianapolis, April, 1875, a number of ladies, delegates from their missionary societies, assembled and organized a presbyterial society. Thirteen societies were reported to them as organized within the bounds of the presbytery. Upon invitation of the Ladies' Presbyterial Society, the Woman's Board of the North-west met in Indianapolis, April, 1876. The meeting of this board, through the presence of the Spirit of the Lord, was a glorious occasion, and great good was accomplished. The ladies are quietly but earnestly pursuing their work in the different churches, meeting also in their presbyterial society at the time of the stated meetings of presbytery.

REVIVALS.

Every year since 1870 there have been revivals in some of the churches of the presbytery. The year of 1872–'73 seemed to be most barren of results in the conversion of souls and additions to the churches. The year of 1873–'74 was a year of revivals, and additions were made in goodly numbers to many of the churches. The year of 1874–'75 was also a year of blessing, and still more signally the year of 1875–'76. During this last named year six hundred and sixty-one were added to the churches on profession of faith. The next largest accession to the churches was in 1873–'74, when five hundred and two were added on profession of faith. The least number added was in the year 1872–'73, when two hundred and twenty were added on profession of faith.

PROGRESS.

One church a year has been added since 1870 to the roll of the churches of presbytery. All of these churches have a promising future. Five are in Indianapolis. One, the Memorial Church, is already one of the strong churches of the presbytery. Several new church buildings have been erected. According to the United States census report the value of church property held in 1860 by the Presbyterian churches within the bounds of the present presbytery, was a little less than $150,000. The estimated value of property now held by the churches is about $600,000.

During the last six years, the churches have received into their communion, upon profession of their faith, two thousand four hundred and seventy-six (2,476) members, and by letter, one thousand eight hundred and fifteen (1,815.) The present membership of the church is five thousand eight hundred and nineteen (5,819,) an increase in membership since 1870, of more than thirty-three per cent. The number of churches is thirty-eight, the number of ministers forty. Of these ministers ten are without charge, some by reason of the infirmities of age, others for other reasons. One is a Professor in the State University, another is a Foreign Missionary. The effective ministerial force of the presbytery, is twenty-eight ministers. The field is rich and will become richer and more productive with cultivation. It is the central region of the State in which it lies. From Indianapolis, the Capital of the State, streams of influence will go forth constantly to all parts of the State. And through the great missionary organizations of the church, the influence of this field, in common with that of all other parts of the Presbyterian church in our land, is to go forth into all the world. But in the field itself, there are many spiritual wastes to be made, through the blessing of the Lord upon labor, to blossom as the rose. "Arise, O Lord, into thy rest, thou and the ark of thy strength. Let thy priests be clothed with righteousness, and let thy saints shout for joy."

www.ingramcontent.com/pod-product-compliance
Lightning Source LLC
Chambersburg PA
CBHW022131160426
43197CB00009B/1230